Women's Representations from Radical Naturalism to the New Woman Response

A Transatlantic Perspective of European, Latin American, and American Narratives

Dr José F. Rojas-Viana

Louisiana State University

Series in Literary Studies

 VERNON PRESS

www.vernonpress.com

In the Americas:
Vernon Press
1000 N West Street, Suite 1200
Wilmington, Delaware, 19801
United States

In the rest of the world:
Vernon Press
C/Sancti Espiritu 17,
Malaga, 29006
Spain

Series in Literary Studies

Library of Congress Control Number: 2023946589

ISBN: 978-1-64889-791-7

Cover design by Vernon Press using elements designed by Gordon Johnson from Pixabay and aopsan / Freepik.

Table of Contents

Acknowledgments

First, I would like to express my sincere gratitude to a great former tutor and now colleague, Dorota Heneghan, from whom I received great feedback that allowed this project to move forward. The same special thanks should be extended to Sharon Weltman and Alejandro Cortazar. They contributed a great deal to the success of this work, and it was a great honor and pleasure to work with them, too. This project would not have been possible without their assistance. Hence, I am very thankful to my wife, Julia López, my daughter, María Jose Rojas López and her husband, Lance Collasos, for their understanding and support. I cannot finish the list of thankfulness without mentioning Rafael Orozco, who helped me in many ways to get to this point.

Introduction.
The Atlantic Basin and Views of Woman in the Nineteenth Century

The Atlantic Basin is a natural barrier that, once crossed by Europeans, facilitated a series of human contacts rich in transcendental transformations (Thornton 7). Pre- and post-Columbus voyages through the Atlantic were many in number and from different places. They produced continual clashes between world views that influenced and transformed cultures, politics, and history around the world (Thornton 7-8). Navigation through the Atlantic Basin can be marked as early as the thirteenth century, not only by Scandinavians but also by Caribbean inhabitants and later by the Portuguese in their travels to Africa (Thornton 8). From that point in time to the end of the nineteenth century, control of the Atlantic Basin marked the rise and fall of imperial and colonial rules, a significant element for European development. The forced immigration of Africans by Europeans is the darkest example in human history of the cruel colonial transatlantic power on the American continent. This inhuman and transformative practice lasted almost to the early twentieth century (Klein xv).

During the *fin de siècle,* the interest of European empires not only focused on economic growth but also promoted travelers, explorers, and writers in search of scientific, social, and geographical discoveries. These people were usually from England, the United States, or Spain. They crossed the Atlantic for various reasons (Guelke and Morint 306). Transatlantic travel in the nineteenth century was an explosive display of technical, scientific, social, racial, and political changes and perspectives. Literature and science marked many of these advances all over the world and formed a prevailing knowledge highlighting differences among human beings. Women were often the object of a negative differentiation echoed through many disciplines. European, North American and Latin American patriarchal literary works developed and depicted treacherous female characters, which early feminists responded to with creative strategies of opposition. The works analyzed in this book represent not only the reflection of the nineteenth-century view of women as biologically, psychologically, morally, hereditarily, and spiritually different from men but also the mechanisms of repression that helped to maintain these ideas as well as anti-establishment mechanisms that refuted them. By establishing a conversation among these works from different perspectives, this book reveals how deeply rooted the patriarchal intentions to control many aspects of women were and how the New Woman writers reacted to it. These authors intentionally deconstructed the patriarchal model with strong arguments, debunking its substantive theories and positions from science to the political arena. These theoretical positions still resonate today and allow connections to contemporary literature.

This thesis, then, comparatively interprets representations of women within Radical Naturalism and New Woman perspectives from both sides of the Atlantic Basin. Hence, it argues metatheoretically that different constructions of female characters established a gendered dialogue through the themes of the *femme fatale,* alternative spaces, eugenics, and social Darwinism. Despite multiple locations, various languages, and different genders of authorship, the texts of both literary perspectives analyzed here converge in depicting women as submissive victims within patriarchal institutions such as the state, family, or society. However, whereas Radical Naturalism tends to create regressive characters that fall into marginal places, sickness, and death, the New Woman perspective tends to create progressive characters, allowing them to be successful and healthy with an alternative path. The novels that are selected to illustrate this thesis are as follows: *Santa* (1903), by Federico Gamboa from Mexico, *La hija del bandido o los subterráneos del nevado* (1887), by Refugio Barragán de Toscano from Mexico; *Tess of the D'Urbervilles: A Pure Woman* (1891), by Thomas Hardy from Great Britain; *Ideala* (1888), by Sarah Grand from Great Britain; *The Awakening* (1899), by Kate Chopin from the United States; and *La gota de sangre* (1911), *La piedra angular* (1891), and the short story "Tío Terrones" (1920), by Emilia Pardo Bazán from Spain.

Before moving to the analysis of these novels, it might be useful to explain and define some key terms deployed throughout this work. The term Naturalism was coined by Emile Zola, who suggested that writers need to express different perspectives on society as one would do in a scientific study. In their works, these writers generally focus on negative aspects of life and/or marginalities of all kinds to portray mostly female characters as marginal individuals (Ordiz 8). Radical Naturalism refers to an extreme version of naturalistic narrative, as Pura Fernández explains in her "Introducción" to *La prostituta (Novela medico-social)* (1884). The term was made by the Spanish writer Alejandro Sawa to describe a narrative that was also called the brothel novel, *barricada* [barricade], or *novela medico-social* [medico-social novel], as Fernández points out. This narrative usually has social, political, and medical perspectives and tends to bring all the events to the extreme, affecting the main character, often a woman. The New Woman was a literary and social trend in the 1890s (Rich 1). In her book *New Woman Fiction: Women Writing First-Wave Feminism,* Ann Heilmann defines this concept as follows:

> Who or what was the New Woman? A literary construct, a press fabrication and discursive marker of rebellion, or a 'real' woman? A writer, social reformer, or feminist activist? A middle-class daughter eager to study for a career, a married woman chafing against legal inequality, a woman-loving spinster, a reluctant mother, a sexual libertarian? Even the factual writers who defined and were defined as New Women were apt to shift and contest the parameters of the category... (2)

This multifaceted feminist movement that appeared at the turn of the nineteenth century took up a prominent place in the literature of the time. The quote above helps with the understanding of the New Woman depictions in the novels mentioned above. In addition, the definition facilitates the comparisons with the works from Spain and Mexico, allowing one to gather similarities and differences from their counter part from the United States and England.

Crime was defined as an act against criminal laws and/or civil laws. Deviancy was seen as sexual behavior that went beyond the code of social norms, and that was controlled by society and by the state's normativity. For example, prostitution was often considered not only a deviant behavior but also a crime in many countries during the nineteenth century. This book, thus, uses these terms (Radical Naturalism, New Woman, crime, and deviancy) to support its main arguments. Atavism is a term that changed over time, but in the timeframe that concerns this work, it was defined as the tendency of a human being to show physical, psychological, or social regressions toward an animal state. This concept involved the individual's genealogical past and future generations (Seitler 2-5). The term has a racial dimension, and it was used in the field of eugenics to explain human differences. The term served for different purposes. More specifically, it served to emphasize alterity. It was also very close to the concept known as social Darwinism, which refers to the connections between Darwin's evolution theory and social settings. This concept was coined by Herbert Spencer to cruelly provide the upper social classes with the idea that the one who survives is better than poor and marginalized individuals who might, therefore, perish (Lewis 155). Social Darwinism was part of positivism, related to social structures, and was practiced not only in social contexts but also in politics across the globe (Lewis 155). These two terms help to frame the conversations in Chapter 3, in which I discuss Hardy's and Gamboa's novels in a multicultural context and Transatlantic view.

Foucault explains the concepts of "discourse" and "bio-power." He defines the former as a mechanism that controls individuals or masses through a series of strategies and/or methods that deliver organization and distribute power to direct or redirect society's expected understanding of the triggered events.

Examples of this discourse is the criminalization of homosexuality and other sexuality-related issues. He also defines bio power as "what brought life and its mechanism into the realm of the explicit calculations and made knowledge-power an agent of transformation of human life" (Foucault, "Bio-Power" 265). Nonetheless, and most importantly for this work, he accurately shows how patriarchal dominance takes the form of the state in place of the king and how bio-power purposely delivers a kind of control throughout a series of created institutions and methods. In Chapters 1 and 3, these two Foucauldian terms illustrate how the medical discourse appears in the *femme fatale* as a moral device and how social and biological sciences constructed a sketch of the late nineteenth-century woman. The *femme fatale* is a universally known term that the Oxford Dictionary defines as a "very beautiful woman that men find sexually attractive who brings them trouble or unhappiness ...." This term became important to the following analysis, with the caveat that here the term itself will be explored to the extension of the unhappiness and damage for the *femme fatale*.

The analysis of the mentioned novels and short stories comes from three major inquiries. The first inquiry intends to search for differences or similarities in the representation of women as deviant/criminal from the perspectives of Radical Naturalism and the New Woman in the model of the *femme fatale* used by Gamboa, Pardo Bazán, Grand, Chopin, and Hardy and how they creatively used the same theme across the Atlantic Basin. The second inquiry questions how the spaces of the brothel, the cave, the countryside, the house, and inns help to frame the female characters according to Radical Naturalism and the New Woman's points of view. The third and last inquiry deals with the characters of Tess and Santa and how the themes of eugenics, atavism, and social Darwinism unveil not only cultural nodes between these two literatures but also social questions. These inquiries are supported by different theories that will help explain the unique comparative analysis of criminal and deviant female characters. So, in the following chapters, the texts in this work are reviewed from different theoretical frameworks.

Literature deals with all aspects of the human being, and it often reflects the organic nature of life events. For that reason, different theoretical perspectives help to support and to explain how to interpret the disparate events and characters depicted in these novels and short stories. Moreover, the objective of these theoretical and philosophical frameworks is to consider the patriarchal discourse of control and dominance in the literary representation of deviant women in the late nineteenth century on both sides of the Atlantic Basin. They also explore definitions of deviancies and criminality in women from the social and biological sciences present in the abovementioned narratives. These theoretical positions allow us to understand how the representation of space helps to frame women with different discursive purposes. Lastly, these philosophical positions contextualize the differences of culture reflected in the texts from both sides of the Atlantic.

Theoretical and Philosophical Framework

In the Transatlantic perspective, the principle of multiplicity appears in the idea of the rhizome and suggests that "multiplicity" as a substance creates different relations of one with its world (Deleuze and Guattari 226). In other words, multiplicity is a rhizomatic or rhizome-like concept that expresses itself as a tree-like structure, allowing it to increase itself in number while changing its nature. It is neither object nor subject, and it moves on a plane in a line that can be interrupted but not destroyed entirely. Nazism can be a good example of a rhizome-like structure (Deleuze and Guattari 227-228). The Transatlantic examination here highlights the chronological discrepancies represented in the novels analyzed here. The rhizome-type connections reverberate along nature and culture. It also finds a niche in Northrop Frye's literary theory of the archetype. The archetype shows how mythical tropes appear iteratively in all literatures and cultures throughout time (Frye 137-138). Examples that include the trope of the hero and the trope of the pilgrimage appear in Homer's works and later reappear in many other texts. The hero and the pilgrim figures allow one to see different rhizomatic juxtapositions as they take shape in different forms and styles used from earlier narratives and even to present-day literature. All these observations apply to the novels of Hardy, Gamboa, Grand, Pardo Bazán, Barragán de Toscano, and Chopin. Another good resemblance of multiplicity as rhizome-like appears in the works of Giles, Slettedahl, Manning, and Taylor, supporting the argument that the Atlantic is an element that creates disparate literary productions and cultures. The Atlantic Basin also acts as a plane of multiple dimensions and conveys a multiplicity of connections.

Susan Manning and Andrew Taylor examine the prominent place of the comparisons of texts from both sides of the Atlantic. This field developed during the Cold War era. It is a line of research that comes from American studies, US-based scholarship in which the political position of the United States intersected with literary studies (Manning and Taylor 4-5). This situation raised political and geographical questions about the role of the United States as a device of integration within British literary discussions. Their main point is that comparisons are entangled with political views from "trans- and post-nationalist" (4) perspectives that include the study of the multicultural environment across the Atlantic. Transatlantic studies not only cover geographical places but also expand and intersect greatly with other disciplines, including comparative literature. The dimension of gender has made important contributions to dialogues in the forms of texts and intertextualities that come from both shores of the Atlantic, which mark a multiplicity of epistemological connections (Slettedahl- Macpherson 5). Paul Giles revises the historical, literary, cultural, and philosophical contrasts between both sides of the Atlantic. The Atlantic Basin was, and is, an active place for literary dialogues, particularly between the United States and Great Britain. The existence of the false idea of literary homogeneity in the United States is within the collective imaginary. In reality, the multiplicity of cultures reacted differently to literary texts, particularly during the nineteenth century (Giles 16). These premises set the stage for my analysis, particularly for the novels discussed in Chapter 3, which compares the texts in the Mexican and British literary contexts.

Michael Foucault's works are vital to explaining different mechanisms used by the power (patriarchal, state, or other power) depicted in the fiction covered in this study. For example, in *Santa,* the house is not only the space used to depict the family dynamics but also the resemblance of the famous panopticon. Foucault explains the importance of *fin de siècle* philosophies, social sciences, and biological sciences and how they entangled with patriarchal dominance to control society. Different mechanisms of control developed in the early eighteenth century were more effective and numerous in the nineteenth century. Control was delivered, he points out, by two mechanisms. On the one hand, the term "hierarchical observations" refers to a constructed mechanism that uses the space to see differences among individuals, a control device (Foucault, *Discipline & Punish* 170-173). For example, windows or patios were sometimes made specifically to observe spaces such as classrooms, military barracks, or hospitals. This was an effective tool for demarking the differences among the individuals in such institutions. Similarly, Foucault explains the term "normalizing judgment" as a mechanism that comes after the observations, one in which individuals (e.g., students, workshop workers, and so forth) were judged according to a series of norms marked by boundaries of behavior or performance. This was a disciplinary power delivered by humiliation, minor depravations, or physical punishment (Foucault, *Discipline & Punish* 178).

The process of normalization has become a matter of discussion since the late nineteenth century's scientific reasoning included women in a taxonomical category in order to normalize their image and gain total control over them. Furthermore, Foucault reveals the effectiveness of the normalization strategy as he states, "The examination combines the techniques of observing hierarchy and those of normalizing judgment. It is a normalizing gaze, a surveillance that makes it possible to qualify, to classify, and to punish" (*Discipline & Punish* 184). In the process of normalization throughout these mechanisms, discipline appears in the form of power. These explanations contribute to this book's discussion of the abnormal view of women at the time.

In addition, Foucault theorizes heterotopic spaces and suggests that there are at least six principles through which the heterotopic space can manifest itself. One example is the forbidden spaces into which the individual is separated because of a crisis (Foucault, "Of Other Spaces" 4). Society constructs a special space for these individuals out of the norm and under the view of the nineteenth-century sciences. So psychiatric hospitals, prisons, or even special places in schools were designed with the purpose of enclosing deviants or criminals in general, but in this case, the literary works include women. I examine these aspects of space in Chapter 2.

In his essay "Of Other Spaces," Foucault explains the heterotopias and their six principles.[1] His ideas about these principles are applicable to the interpretation of the spaces in *Santa* and *Tess of the D'Urbervilles* as well as in Pardo Bazán's novels. For example, in *Santa*, the reader sees the brothel as one end of society, and in "Tío Terrones," the rural town is on the other side of civilization. These narratives use heterotopias to frame some characters in marginal situations in which crime or deviancies are present, while some authors use them to express disconformity with society. Foucault, no doubt, provides an explanation of how these nineteenth-century agencies and formulas of control are relevant and how they resonate in today's society. The importance of Foucault's epistemology can be explained considering the concept of a deconstructive act in Jacques Derrida's "Letter to a Japanese Friend" described as follows:

> ...deconstruction is neither an *analysis* nor a *critique*... It is not an analysis in particular because the dismantling of a structure is not a regression toward a *simple element*, toward an *indissoluble origin*. These values, like that of analysis, are themselves philosophemes subject to deconstruction. No more is it a critique, in general sense or in Kantian sense. The instance of apparatus of *kritein* or of *krisis* (decision, choice, judgement, discernment) is itself, as is all the apparatus of transcendental

---

[1] A summary of the six principles of Foucault can be enumerated as follow: The first principle suggests that all the cultures develop heterotopias. The second principle states that each heterotopia can have different functions. The third principle explains that a heterotopia can exist in a juxtaposing real space. The four principle suggest that every heterotopia is related to segments of time while open or close according its function. The fifth principle states that heterotopia is not free accessible as public places. Finally, the sixth principle explains that every heterotopia interacts with the external space creating ideal organized or messy spaces.

critique, one of the essential "themes" or "objects" of deconstruction. (3; Emphasis in original)[2]

Foucauldian concepts illuminate the texts that I am using here, as they reflect many aspects of daily life in the late nineteenth and early twentieth centuries. This epistemological notion explains how the aforementioned novels depict women.

Similarly, Pierre Bourdieu explains the concept of the "field of cultural production" and how the state, the economy, the producer, and the artist play a fundamental role as an apparatus of power (Bourdieu 77). A work of art (e.g., a painting, a sketch, an essay, a work of fiction, or a musical score) participates with its creator in the distribution of the field of power by economic means. The concept of "the creator of creators" in artistic production during the nineteenth century is an important part of the articulation of power (Bourdieu 77-78). According to this concept, the artist is a part of the dominant class of individuals. Looking at this dimension, one can see how texts reflect these instances in the characterization of life in which the economy also acts as a state's force to control society or individuals (Bourdieu 78). For example, the narrative events in Gamboa's novel allow the reader to see how this author becomes the voice of the dominant class. This work, then, takes all the above theoretical premises as a point of departure for the attempt at comparative interpretations of the texts and perspectives mentioned.

From Radical Naturalism to the New Woman Response

Vital to my analysis is Zola, who reminds us that "...the naturalistic novel is simply an inquiry in nature, beings, and things ..." (*The Experimental Novel* 123). Zola insists of writing, "[T]his dream of the physiologist and the experimental doctor is also of the novelist, who employs the experimental method in his study of man as a simple individual and as a social animal" (25). Similarly, Cesare Lombroso (1835-1909) studies the topic of criminal men and women from the perspective of biological science (Rafter and Gibson 3). All his works became influential in the nineteenth century, particularly his work on criminal women. Additionally, he developed a theory related to the "atavistic offender" that discussed the retrogression of the criminal individual's mind and body to primitive stages (Rafter and Gibson 3). Zola's and Lombroso's views are important to my analysis in that they enable us to understand nineteenth-

---

[2] I am using this quote as a commentary on Foucault's epistemology, which I see as the construction of an ideological binary that helps to debunk concepts, diagnostics, devices, and thoughts to create a new view that allows one to see their purposes in terms of power or dominance.

century thought about depictions of criminal women, which I use throughout my discussion. Following Zola's writings, Radical Naturalism illustrates the manner in which this literary trend presents the woman. The treatment of the main character represents the social oppression toward women who are outside of the normality. As mentioned above, in Gamboa's text, prostitution becomes the only way for such a woman, which brings the events to the extreme for the woman's character and her surroundings.

Also, I bring to the surface across the chapters the way in which these feminist works sparked comparative discussions. The New Woman was certainly a multifaceted literary movement. The New Woman perspective was ambiguous in the United States and had race nuances. While some writers showed racial bias toward white women, other writers desired progress for black women. The English novelist Marie Louise de la Ramée or Ouida criticized the New Woman. She argued that the movement put much emphasis on women as victims of men and that they should see them as victims of women, too. Ouida, with her pessimistic criticism, certainly highlights some weak aspects of the New Woman that will help the movement to grow and progress. Nonetheless, Sarah Grand, one of the pioneers of the New Woman perspective, in her essay "Does Marriage Hinder A Woman's Self-Development?" discusses how women should be granted independence whether they are married or not. This was a critical point at the end of the nineteenth century, when she stated, "… the man is dragged down enough; but he, by the customs of society, can escape to a large extent from the dead weight of his self-inflicted destiny.… To the woman, as always, society, having been ordered by a man, has not been quite so kind" (119). Grand directed the attention toward the opposition between males and females and highlighted the inescapable subalternity of the woman at her time. Similarly, Emilia Pardo Bazán expressed her concerns about the violence against women in Spain throughout several essays written in the magazine "La Ilustración Artística." As Grand, Pardo Bazán addressed gender disparate relations as she suggests the advantages for men in all aspects of daily life are unequal to women. Furthermore, she analyzed the criminal law in regard to married men who killed their wives, who were not usually punished for it. It is important to her to highlight that these similarities can convey the idea of the New Woman in Spain, though the term was not used in this context. It occurs in the same case that Nancy LaGreca notices in her book and shows us how Refugio Barragán de Toscano in *La hija* presents the main character and the Angel of the House who resolves and restores the order in the 1700s Mexican countryside. The character indeed shows the progressive ideas of Barragán de Toscano toward women in her time. The sense of the New Woman once again is present, at least in the progressive character of María in *La hija*. It is important to highlight that the Angel of the House does not prevent the idea of the New Woman and progress. It is important to notice that in Latin America, the concept of race was ambiguous, and sometimes, it was used to build the nation. From this ambiguous idea, Jose de Vasconcelos, a Mexican writer and philosopher, created the idea of *the cosmic race*. According to Vasconcelos, the fusion of all races in Latin America created a new era that was positive and progress in nation-building. Nonetheless, the indigenous and black people were always relegated to subordinated positions in society. Spain was more inclined to see differences not through race but through social class and regional idiosyncrasies. There was the idea of center and periphery, in which Madrid was the center that had education and progress, and the peripheral regions lacked education and progress. This vision also resonated in Latin America.

Margo Culley shows how the work of Kate Chopin, *The Awakening*, attracted a great deal of feminist criticism from the mid-twentieth century and how these critics brought to the forefront themes such as marriage, power, or patriarchy. The main character of Chopin's novel no doubt shows a clear resistance to unequal marriage and shows empowerment of the woman. It also shows the capability of the woman to react toward oppression. These women authors and characters, without a dispute, present a pattern that conveys the idea of the New Woman, as defined above. It seems to be a collective response toward other depictions of the woman, as in the Radical Naturalism of Federico Gamboa. Nonetheless, in many of the arguments of these women writers, the readers will find depictions of the Victorian visual culture, as Bram Dijkstra points out.

During the nineteenth century, different depictions of women were the subject of erotic fantasies, and female figures were considered dangerous in many forms (Dijkstra 85). For example, the "sleeping women" in paintings were interpreted as a fantasy of women who surrendered to the male will; however, these depicted women were interpreted as dangers nonetheless (Dijkstra 80). Toril Moi contends that early feminism in England underlined sex-gender distinctions and served as a framework for late feminists such as Simone de Beauvoir and poststructuralists' perspectives on gender. The woman's body and the relevant function of biology in the late nineteenth century brought to light the machinery of science to control society and the patriarchal discourse on women (Moi 15). Dijkstra's and Moi's arguments explain how women's portrayals in these works are subjected to the *fin de siècle* liberal bourgeois male perspective. Although this book deals with topics such as feminism, gender, Naturalism, the New Woman, and Transatlantic studies, the comparisons are specific and unique. Also, this analysis reveals that the patriarchal intentions of control in all aspects of women's lives were deeply rooted. Additionally, this project shows how the New Woman responded to patriarchal dominance in a deconstructive manner with innovative patterns and strong arguments. At the same time, it debunks theories and postures that marked their presence across cultural fields on both sides of the Atlantic. Many authors and scholars have studied the texts and perspectives mentioned here as early as the late nineteenth century.

Issues in Translations

The practice of translation has raised concerns from Saint Augustine to Walter Benjamin. Regarding the difficulty of rendering poems, literature, or laws from one language to another, the problem that has been expressed constantly is the translator himself/herself. The anecdotical phrase of *traduttore traditore* [3] speaks clearly to the arduous and difficult task of the translation. Jorge Luis Borges chronologically compares a series of translations from the version of Jean Antoine Gallard to the German version of Enno Littmann. Borges brings to light how a translation can change from poetry to prose or become an exhaustively footnoted text. Nonetheless, Borges highlights different approaches adopted by translators. For example, he explains Dr. J.C. Mardrus's version as follows:

> In general, it can be said that Mardrus does not translate the book's words but its scenes: a freedom denied to translators, but tolerated in illustrators, who are allowed to add these kinds of details ... I do not know if these smiling diversions are what infuse the work with such a happy air, the air of a far-fetched personal yarn rather than of a laborious hefting of dictionaries. But to me the Mardrus "translation" is the most readable of them all – after Burton's incomparable version which is not truthful either. (106)

Borges's essay shows how dynamic a translation could be and how it might provide us with results that could be deemed good or bad. Walter Benjamin points out that the translator's "task" is "finding that intended effect [*Intention*][4] upon the language into which he is translating which produces in it the echo of the original" (177). Roman Jakobson not only addresses a linguistic perspective and methods of translation but also summarizes the structure of a translation as follows: "translation involves two equivalent messages in two different codes" (183). As one can see, Transatlantic studies intersect with comparative literature in regard to translations. Thus, in the following pages, I attempt a series of translations needed in this work. All translations from Spanish to English in this book are my own unless otherwise stated.

---

[3] In the best of the cases translated "traitor translator."
[4] Emphasis from the source.

The Comparative Literature Field

Although translation is vital for this work as a field that helps with textual analysis, other theoretical fields complement this comparative approach. As John Pizer suggests, the field of comparative literature involves a multiplicity of theoretical perspectives, while it in itself is a theory. This premise explains how this book examines the texts of Gamboa, Hardy, Grand, Pardo Bazán, Barragán de Toscano, Grand, and Chopin from multidimensional perspectives and junctures, while in the background, the analysis is supported by the premises of comparative literature. Therefore, a brief explanation and brief historical background of the field of comparative literature is necessary to understand the complexity of the comparativist task.

Historically, the field of comparative literature originated in France in the 1800s and disseminated across Europe, as D'haen, Domínguez, and Thomsen explain. Nonetheless, these authors suggest that when it came to the United States at the end of World War II, comparative literature installed itself at the center of modern language departments and enlarged its scope in the field of world literature. The contact of both fields consequently affected each other; the texts became not only more numerous but also broader in literary traditions and translations (D'haen, Domínguez, and Thomsen, "Reading Paths" xvi). Vilashini Cooppan illuminates this by showing how comparative literature needed revision in its essential conception and how it theoretically and methodologically works. Cooppan evaluates Goethe's notion of *Weltliteratur* as a concept that not only transgressed national borderlines at the time but also showed linguistic idiosyncrasies and the absence of the major or "great masterworks of prior traditions" (179). Hence, she notices that Goethe's *Weltliteratur* represents early nineteenth-century principles of nationalism as a benevolent intention of spreading literature as a human connection that would spark tolerance among different nations. Overall, Cooppan states, "The history of comparative literature, then, is also to some degree the history of globalization" (179). Most important of all is that she restates one of the main components of comparative literature, that is, its capacity or its intention to make comparisons. In addition, Cooppan points out how the historical method became another aspect of comparative literature: "Our task is then to learn to read the past for its differences from, as well as its similarities to, the present; to locate our ghostly forefathers within their own historical and ideological moment and discern in them the skeleton of a method that might visit us again" (183).

Another important aspect of comparative literature is the concept of circulation, which David Damrosch considers crucial to textual analysis and to a profound study of broad topics in comparative literature in the post-secondary education classroom. Damrosch suggests that world literature is "a mode of circulation and of reading, a mode that is as applicable to individual works as to bodies of material, available for reading established classics and new discoveries alike" (200). In this book, the idea of circulation matters as it deals with works by Hardy, Gamboa, Pardo Bazán, Grand, and Chopin that were widely circulated and taught. Also, this work analyzes a less-circulated text by Pardo Bazán, the short story "Tío Terrones," which paints a different fate for the female character. Moreover, Cooppan allows one to understand the idea of the point of departure from which texts would have their main perspective. She describes it as follows:

> [P]oints of departure may be several and of various kinds ("a semantic interpretation, a rhetorical trope, a syntactic sequence ...")[.] Of the many possible points of departure conceivable for a world literature course, we signaled out two both marked by the *ansatzpunkt's* doubling of location...the practice of reading and the structure of genre. (185)

Of course, both points of departure, she mentions, are important not just for the creation of literature or in the pedagogy of world literature but also for literary analysis. In addition, she offers some examples of how comparative literature works. First, she says that genre is in constant movement, and so "[t]he study of the changing history of literary genres further stands to teach us something about a larger cultural story..." (185). Her second example deals with the wide range of disciplines and perspectives that comparative literature might employ at the same time as the method of a globalizing view: "The drama unit subsequently paired Shakespeare's *Macbeth* with Akira Kurosawa's Japanese film version, *Throne of Blood.* ... These selections restaged the question of cultural differences even while attesting to the transability of certain narratives and narrative forms" (189). Here, Cooppan also highlights the importance of the cultural background. Though the background may be different, the comparisons are not only possible but multiple. Undoubtedly, cultural differences are an important part of the analysis in all the chapters of this work, as they not only give a reflection of nineteenth-century daily life but also unveil the Transatlantic uniqueness of cultural backgrounds.

Corpus Justification

The works that are analyzed here have been chosen for the purpose of comparison. They represent different perspectives and values of the nineteenth century across the Atlantic Basin regarding women. The Mexican *Santa* of Federico Gamboa is the best example of Radical Naturalism and was an exceptional novel in sales during the early twentieth century. The novel brings to the forefront the difficulties of women in the Mexican context at the time. In *La hija* by Refugio Barragán de Toscano, the main character, María, becomes the agent of a positive resolution of the novel's conflict. The works of Emilia Pardo Bazán are not only the best representation of Spanish women's literature, but they give the female characters an important and progressive role. By positioning her characters in such a way, Pardo Bazán is projecting a positive image of women's role in society. The works of Gamboa, Barragán the Toscano, and Emilia Pardo Bazán, then, will facilitate a comparison between male and female writing and representations across the Atlantic in Spanish literature. The same occurs with the works of Kate Chopin, Sarah Grand, and Thomas Hardy. Kate Chopin in *The Awakening* shows a woman who liberates herself from her marriage. In *Ideala*, Sarah Grand also presents a woman in the process of leaving an abusive husband. *Tess*, by Thomas Hardy, is a complex narrative that portrays the socioeconomic problems of rural women in England. All these texts, no doubt, provide enough material for a deep analysis of the representations of women at the end of the nineteenth century in the context of Transatlantic studies. It is important to clarify that this book does not directly analyze racial issues across the Atlantic. The literature works are more inclined to discuss social class differences, center-periphery differences, or socioeconomic status issues rather than race as such.

Geographic Scope, Biographical Background and Plot Summaries

In general, the geographic scope of this book deals with four different countries located on each side of the Atlantic Basin, allowing Transatlantic comparisons. Each country evolved differently due to colonialism, imperialism, wars, and other causes. In the late nineteenth century, Mexico, Spain, Great Britain, and the United States showed a stylistic disparity in literary production, particularly from the perspectives of Radical Naturalism and the New Woman. This disparity allows one to study asynchronous literary works from the *fin de siècle* period and helps to put on display historical convergences, as well as obvious differences. For example, positivistic ideology marked its presence in different years in the Americas, from the United States through Argentina, as well as in Spain and Great Britain. This cultural trend became part of the biological and social science discourse that served as a device to control society. History shows how the British Empire struggled economically while expanding. Additionally, the Spanish Empire suffered great economic erosion by 1898 after the Spanish-American War, in which Spain lost its last three colonies: Guam, Cuba, and Puerto Rico.

In Mexico, the *porfiriato* was a period of a conservative dictatorship ruled by Porfirio Díaz (1830–1915). This period lasted from 1877 through 1911. It was a period in which positivism and the nation-building project were active and guided by Díaz under the motto of "estabilidad y progreso" [progress and stability]. This cultural vision is also reflected, in one way or another, in the narratives of Gamboa and Barragán de Toscano. Gamboa was born in Mexico City in 1864. Gamboa was a very versatile person. He started as a gazette writer and, in 1888, became a diplomat. He climbed the political ladder as the minister of exterior relations, and by 1913, he had become the secretary of exterior relations. Gamboa died while serving as the director de la Academia Mexicana de la lengua [director of the Academy of the Spanish Language of Mexico]. His main work, *Santa*, was widely known in Mexico. Later, the novel was adapted to the screen. The film, directed by Antonio Moreno, was popular in Latin America. The novel is considered one of the most representative of the Radical Naturalism perspective.

In Gamboa's novel, the circular narrative mostly focuses on its main character, Santa. The story begins with Santa, portrayed as a rural girl who lives in the little town of Chilamistac. She falls in love with a captain of the Mexican army. This event marks the point of her misfortune. First, she gets pregnant. Then, she is expelled from her house by her mother and brothers. The last event eventually leads her into prostitution, alcoholism, sickness, and death.

The Mexican author Refugio Barragán de Toscano had already achieved a prominent and popular place in Mexican literature by the second half of the nineteenth century. Her life began in Tonila, Mexico, in 1843. The Barragán family lived in that town and later in Colima, Mexico. They lived a modest life, and they managed to save money for education. Refugio was educated according to Catholic values with the objective of becoming a good mother and wife. In her teenage years, she published poetry. Later, she studied education and worked as a teacher. She married Esteban Toscano, an educator, and lived in Guadalajara, Mexico. After her husband died, she had to work as a teacher and as a writer. Her works are vast and range from novels, poems, and short stories to literary criticism. In her writings, she joins the voice of other women writers in the quest to be part of the literary landscape dominated by male production (Zalduono xiii).

In Barragán de Toscano's *La hija del bandido*, the narrative constructs a world from a bandit's cave, although it focuses on the main character, María, framing her in a colonial Mexican historical period. María is a heroine who restores the original place of the things in the narrative universe. She is raised in a bandit's world (as her father is a bandit). María must not only restore the original place of things but also fight on the side of the law. She overcomes her father's omnipresent power and defeats him. Later, María meets Rafael, with whom she falls in love. Influenced greatly by Catholicism during Mexico's colonial period, the story redirects María's fate. Although the resolution for the character is positive, she renounces her marriage to Rafael to become a nun.

Emilia Pardo Bazán was a prolific writer during the second half of the nineteenth century and the early twentieth century. She was born in 1851 into an aristocratic family in Galicia, Spain, though she spent many years in Madrid. She learned how to read and write early in her childhood. Her passion for literature during her lifetime is well known. Pardo Bazán married José Fernando Quiroga in 1868 at the age of seventeen. She worked for many journals, newspapers, and magazines in which she expressed concerns about women's role in society. Later, she became a national icon. Her works are numerous, and they include short stories, novels, and literary criticism. Because she was a woman, she was not admitted to the Spanish Royal Academy. Nonetheless, the minister of public instruction (Ministerio de Instrucción Pública) created the chair of contemporary literature at Universidad Central for her. She was not only one of the greatest Spanish writers of her time but also a controversial figure because she was a woman (Sainz de Robles 33). She died in 1921.

In Pardo Bazán's *La piedra angular*, the reader finds an intricate plot in which the male presence is overwhelming. It is the story of a town in which Doctor Moragas, the main character, gets involved in the investigation of a crime committed by a woman. At the same time, we learn about Juan Rojo, the town executioner and an alcoholic who is rejected by everyone (including his wife) because of his job. In addition, the story includes Juan Rojo's son, who is like his father and was socially rejected, lonely, and shy. Women in the story lack their own voices. Readers know them only from the male narrator's perspective. The death penalty is a dilemma to be resolved by men. And Moragas resolves the dilemma by convincing Juan Rojo not to execute the *parricida*.

Crime is the main issue in *La gota de sangre*. A man has been murdered, and Selva, the main character and narrator, solves the crime. The homicide takes place in an aristocratic neighborhood, where Selva investigates the dead body. He finds that the murder has occurred in the house of Julia Fernandina (Chulita Ferna), who is a fallen woman in love with Andrés Ariza, the murderer. As Selva examines the case, the reader learns that Ariza has killed the man because of Ariza's gambling problem, and Julia Fernandina is his accomplice. She has helped Ariza because she is in love with him. Interestingly, instead of punishing her, Selva frees her.

In the short story "Tío Terrones," the reader finds a family of three sisters and a father in a little town far away from Madrid, Spain. The father is known as Tío Terrones by everyone in the town. He expelled his own daughter, Petronilla, from his house because of rumors about her. It was said that his daughter had an affair with a man. She leaves the house, stays for a while in the town, and goes to Madrid, where she makes a living. Later, the narrative line suggests that she got married to a prosperous man. After a couple of years, she returns to the town, but not to her house. She is now prosperous, married, with money and a desire to buy land and a business. Her arrival in the town attracts her siblings and Tío Terrones' attention. This event sparks a series of dialogues between Tío

Terrones and his other daughters, questioning her new position and how she became rich. These conversations, at the end of the story, fade out, leaving Tío Terrones and his other daughters frustrated and wanting to participate in Petronilla's fortune.

Sarah Grand was born in Ireland in 1850 and was the daughter of a former naval officer. She married at the age of sixteen and traveled widely with her husband. By the late nineteenth and early twentieth centuries, she was also well known for women's advocacy, evident in her novels *Ideala* and *The Heavenly Twins* (1893) (Christensen 34). In addition, Grand wrote a great deal of essays and non-fiction texts in support of women. At the beginning of the twentieth century, she joined the suffrage movement and became a member of the Women Writers' Suffrage League. By 1920, she became the assistant of the Mayor of Bath. Grand traveled to the United States, where she gave lectures. She died in 1943 (Christensen 34).

In Grand's *Ideala*, a male narrator presents the protagonist, Ideala, who is mistreated by her husband. She eventually divorces him, which presents a social problem for her. She has the opportunity to explain why she needs to divorce him, but she is socially ignored. Later, she finds out that she is sick, though the reader has no access to her diagnosis, and she finds a lover. Eventually, Ideala decides to end her relationship and help other women, some of whom have marital problems and others engage in prostitution. She does resolve the main concerns of the novel, which are marriage and the social position of women. This character overcomes all the barriers that life puts in front of her, whether socially or biologically.

In his book *The Complete Critical Guide to Thomas Hardy*, Geoffrey Harvey gives an exceptional account of Hardy's life. As Harvey points out, Thomas Hardy was born in 1840 in rural Dorset, England, a region located in the south of the country, from which he created the Wessex space. His interest in reading and writing was possible because his parents promoted these activities at home. He went to school in Stinsford, later into a nonconformist school in Dorchester, and to a "commercial academy" where he received a very good education. Hardy was employed by John Hicks as an assistant working in architecture. Later, in London, he earned prizes in this field. While in London, he contemplated the chance to write. He started publishing short stories and essays in 1879. He soon became an established author. He married Emma Gifford in 1874, though he fell in love with other women during his marriage. As during the reign of Queen Victoria, social class strata were strictly enforced, Hardy was socially and economically deeply affected by this structure. He reflects on social issues under the Victorian strictness of social strata in many of his works. Thomas Hardy's writings are vast and complex. He penned essays, short stories, and novels, but the last period of his life was dedicated to poetry. He died in 1928.

Hardy's novel *Tess of the D'Urbervilles* presents the story of the main character, Tess Durbeyfield (D'Urbervilles), in several "phases". In the first phase, Hardy lays down the geographical settings, the history of the name of D'Urbervilles, and presents the background of the main character, Tess. The reader then sees an innocent, beautiful, and good rural girl and his family. Also, the novel presents other important characters: Tess's family, Angel Clare, a future husband, and the Stoc-D'Urbervilles family, Alec and his mother. As the plot develops, it shows how the death of the family horse is an event that leads to Tess's disgrace. This event helps her mother and father's desire to send Tess to work with the D'Urbervilles, which creates the main problem of the novel. Tess has the chance to participate in countryside gatherings, one in which Tess is sexually assaulted by Alec D'Urbervilles. In the subsequent chapters, we see the consequences of Alec's actions. Tess gets pregnant; while this is noticed, she works hard in countryside labor. The day the baby, Sorrow, is born, he dies. Between two and three years later, she leaves the family's house one more time and goes to Blackmoor to work in a milking house as a dairymaid. During this time, she meets Angel Clare, and the two spend time together while working and after work. She marries Angel, who quickly separates from her because she tells him the truth about her past. After working in the countryside of Wessex, she finds Alec one more time. He promises her many things, but at some point, Tess kills him. This event seals her fate because she is hunted and executed at the end. It is important to mention that during the story, Tess becomes a positive character, but she cannot resolve the main problem.

Emily Thoth studies Kate Chopin's life in her essay "A New Bibliographical Approach" and her book *Kate Chopin*. Chopin was born in St. Louis, Missouri, in 1850 as Katherine O'Flaherty. She was the only sibling who lived past the age of twenty-five. As a Catholic, she went to the Sacred Heart Academy located in St. Louis. In 1870, she married Oscar Chopin, a plantation owner. After a fancy honeymoon in Europe, they settled in New Orleans, Louisiana, between 1870 and 1879. They also moved to Natchitoches, Louisiana. Although married, she claimed her independence in many ways. For example, she used to smoke cigarettes, an activity reserved almost exclusively for males at the time. After Oscar's death, Chopin had to manage the family business. Later, she returned to St. Louis with her mother. She started as a writer in 1889 with the publication of a short story. She continued publishing short stories, essays, and novels. She maintained friendships with female and male poets, journalists, and writers. Chopin's controversial novel *The Awakening* became part of the South's greatest writings. She died in St Louis in 1904. In what follows, I summarize the chapters of this book to provide background for the analysis of criminal and/or deviant female characters contextualized in the nineteenth century.

The Awakening brings to the fore Edna Pontellier, a character who lives on a plantation in Louisiana. She, as the narrator explains, notices that her life is static. She challenges the social norms by ignoring them and creates her own independence in many ways. Edna not only is sexually active with other men as part of her defiance but also challenges other social norms. For example, Madame Ratignolle advises her, "You seem to act without certain amount of reflection which is necessary in this life… Well, the reason— you know how evil-minded the world is…" (91). Finally, Edna kills herself, though this event has no clear explanation.

Chapter Summaries

Chapter 1 deals with the *femme fatale* and the ways in which the New Woman challenged female characters. This chapter also discusses works across the Atlantic in which deviancies and/or criminalities are inscribed in the female characters. It addresses comparisons between Radical Naturalism and the New Woman perspectives in narratives such as *La piedra angular,* "Tio Terrones," *La hija, Santa, The Awakening, Tess,* and *Ideala.* This Chapter focuses on comparing different aspects of Santa, the main character of Gamboa's novel, with the female characters in other novels. Different from Santa is Petronila in "Tío Terrones," Pardo Bazán's short story, who is a successful woman with money despite being beaten and expelled from her house by her father. Similarly, Tess, in Hardy's novel, is a strong woman who survives indifference, hard conditions, and abuses. Ideala, in Grand's novel, recuperates from a divorce, sickness, and social underestimation. Chulita Ferna in *La gota de sangre* can continue with her life despite her involvement in a crime. Baseless accused in *La piedra angular,* an unnamed character is condemned to capital punishment that never takes place. Lastly, in *La hija* by Barragán de Toscano, María is a heroine full of virtues. Edna Pontellier in *The Awakening,* of Chopin, successfully frees herself from a bad marriage and from social constraints.

Chapter 2 explores the importance of alternative spaces, liminal space and subjects, and the social death of female characters in novels by Gamboa, Barragán de Toscano, Pardo Bazán, Hardy and Chopin. The chapter analyzes how the spaces of the house, the cave, the brothel, the countryside, and inns help to frame representations of crime and deviancies in female characters and how the same space and marginalities interact with liminality and with the concept of social death. This chapter argues that Radical Naturalism and the New Woman perspectives negotiated these spaces to highlight the female character's deviancies, crime, or liminality. This chapter discusses the house in *Santa, Tess, The Awakening, La hija,* and *La gota de Sangre.* This element is articulated differently in all these novels, but in general, it is a safe place for the female character. *Santa* the brothel is an ambiguous place that is sometimes safe for the main character but is also dangerous. Other spaces facilitate crime and/or abuse; for example, in *Tess* and *Santa*, the countryside allows many abuses from patriarchal domination. The cave in *La hija* is a place in which crime lives, but María is the heroine who transforms this. Different spaces frame in different ways all these characters.

In Chapter 3, I discuss the themes of eugenics and atavism in connection to alcohol, which is used as a device to explain deviancies and social Darwinism in female characters in *Santa* and *Tess of the D'Urbervilles*. Social Darwinism appears more evident in *Santa* since the main character lacks opportunities to progress. Although both novels differ in many aspects, they converge in the death of the main characters. Nonetheless, Santa and Tess diverge a great deal; while Tess is resilient, healthy, and strong, Santa is the opposite. Gamboa's main character is sick, weak, and physically and mentally deteriorating throughout the novel. Both novels raise deep gender and social concerns in the social context of the Victorian and the Mexican *porfiriato* eras. Additionally, both authors used Naturalism aesthetics in different ways. While Gamboa's narrative emulates Zola's Naturalism, which focuses on the deviancies of society and individuals, Hardy's story, *Tess*, does not strictly follow the same model.

Chapter 1

Women Across the Atlantic: Perspectives of Radical Naturalism and the New Woman Response

The perspective of women at the end of the nineteenth century varies, but gender difference was well marked. Nonetheless, the idea of women as problematic beings was common many times, leading to views of them as predeterminate deviant beings. Certainly, different discourses toward women during the nineteenth century were well-positioned by different disciplines in the fields of social and natural sciences. Radical Naturalism highlighted the deterministic idea of women as naturally, or prone, to becoming deviant. Zola's thought about social recreation drew a literary model in which female characters appear as aberrant beings. During the early and mid-nineteenth century, a growing fear of women's emancipation was cross-culturally present and lasted until the early to mid-twentieth century (Showalter 3). As Ann Heilmann points out in her book *New Woman Fiction*, the social and political struggles and transformations of the *fin de siècle* in crisis were the breeding ground for new philosophical proposals, visions, and positions that had an emphasis on women. In this environment, the idea of the New Woman arose as a new alternative in literary works in Mexico, England, Spain, and the United States, questioning the notion of women as anomalous individuals (Showalter 3).

In what follows, I examine how literary works of the New Woman from both sides of the Atlantic challenged Radical Naturalism's representations of a woman as a deviant and as a *femme fatale*. The works included are Emilia Pardo Bazán's *La piedra angular* (1891) and "Tio Terrones" (1920), Refugio Barragán de Toscano's *La hija del bandido o los subterráneos del nevado* (1887), Federico Gamboa's *Santa* (1903), Kate Chopin's *The Awakening* (1899), Thomas Hardy's *Tess of the D'Urbervilles* (1891), and Sarah Grand's *Ideala* (1888).

Definitions

Before addressing the analysis of these novels, it is important to clarify some terms for understanding the diversity of cultures from Mexico, the United States, Spain, and Great Britain. Pura Fernández defines Radical Naturalism as the depiction of real people by novel writers while hiding their real identities behind fictional characters. This term comes from Zola's idea of Naturalism, but Radical Naturalism overemphasizes how nature works in the characters. The New Woman perspective can be seen as a social, political, and gender critique highlighting women's sexual and intellectual independence (Showalter 37). The *porfiriato*, as John Brushwood points out, was the period between 1877 and 1911 in which the political situation was under the regime of President Porfirio Díaz, who put the country under a dictatorship that affected its social, political, and cultural landscape. Díaz controlled the country under the motto of "estabilidad y progreso" [stability and progress]. Under his dictatorship, positivism dominated all aspects of daily life (Brushwood 379). Lastly, the term femme *fatale* is explained in more detail during the discussion of this chapter below; nonetheless, the term itself became a type of expression of the man's perception of women at the time in Mexico, Spain, the United States, and Great Britain. Furthermore, in order to offer a better understanding of the arguments below in the context of the late nineteenth century, in the next paragraphs, the reader will find the theoretical framework, which includes gender, Transatlantic, and scientific perspectives of women.

Framework

The many ways to see the women in the late nineteenth and early twentieth centuries vary in different dimensions. The male gaze over women during this period touches different aspects of society and of the state. These aspects are embedded in the concept of women as deviants by nature—ideas that come from the positivist ideology, mostly in notes by August Comte, for example. These constructions were also reinforced by the scientific perspective in which "criminal anthropology" contributed to statistical measurements by Cesare Lombroso and Enrico Ferro, illustrated in their book *The Female Offender* (1895). These perspectives were present not only in France and England but also elsewhere in Europe, though, as mentioned above, with temporal disparities.

Toril Moi suggests that the scientific perspective affected the vision of women during the entire nineteenth century. She points out that according to this vision, women are imprinted with a determined or predetermined physiology and psychology that induces them to be or to act as "inferior" beings. Michel Foucault points out that the construction of the normalization of individuals through disciplinary power involves at least three mechanisms (Foucault, *Discipline & Punish* 184). The first is what Foucault calls "hierarchical observation," which deals with the creation of observational sites and objects (e.g., windows and patios). The second mechanism that Foucault suggests is "normalizing judgment," which involves objects and discipline. As part of this disciplinary system, this mechanism has its own laws and allows specific punishable offenses in a specific context (e.g., a workshop, a school) (Foucault, *Discipline & Punish* 176-177). This disciplinary power is carried by humiliation, minor depravations, or physical petty punishment (Foucault, *Discipline & Punish* 178). It creates rules that draw lines between individuals' differences, highlighting the abnormal. The last mechanism is "examination." In Foucault's words, "The examination combines the techniques of observing hierarchy and those of normalizing judgment. It is a normalizing gaze, a surveillance that makes it possible to qualify, to classify, and to punish" (Foucault, *Discipline & Punish* 183-184). In this context, he defines the term "discipline" as "identified neither with an institution nor with an apparatus; it is a type of power, a modality for its exercise, compromising a whole set of instruments, techniques, procedures, levels of application, targets; it is a 'physics' or an 'anatomy' of power, a technology" (Foucault, *Discipline & Punish* 215). Regarding this normativity and gender differences, Moi's readings of science discuss the predeterminate view of women in the nineteenth century, recalling the intervention of the scientific/medical view and pointing out the great impact of that view on social normativity.

Like Foucault, Moi notes the power that existed in late nineteenth-century science. Women in the late nineteenth century were seen as inferior beings physically, mentally, socially, and politically. They were, from the medical point of view, natural deviants. Even more, women's criminality was seen in terms of sexual deviancies, social pathologies, or madness (Lacey 103). Works such as *The Invention of Hysteria Charcot and the Photographic Iconography of the Salpêtrière* by Didi-Huberman or *Traitê des maladies mentales* by Bénédict Augustine Morel are good examples of the medical perspective. Other authors from the sociology point of view, such as Bentham and Lombroso, shaped the ideology of crime and the construction of the criminal. In the introduction to her book, Akiko Tsuchiya argues that in late-nineteenth-century Spain, women were considered potential deviants. Spain, like other European countries, placed special attention on questions of discipline in criminology, anthropology, and medicine, in which hygiene and other types of discourses of control acted against women (Tsuchiya 6). Tamar Mayer studies the relationship between gender and nation-building in which gender, nationalism, and sexuality interact in a balanced power in which "one gender and one nation" are structured into cultural and sociopolitical institutions (Mayer 5). The position of the male or "hetero-male project" that Mayer sees is powered by many sociopolitical factors, such as militarism, heroism, and, most of all, heterosexuality.

In such a sociopolitical environment, the novel in Spain not only expressed concerns and expectations toward women in general but also conveyed anxieties toward women as socially and politically dangerous (Tsuchiya 6). As Tsuchiya suggests, "all women were to some degree deviant.... [A]nxieties about social instability and disorder, as reflected in the cultural imagination of the period, often centered specifically on the figure of the *female* deviant" (15; emphasis in original). She puts in relief the landscape of criminality and the construction of the deviant in Spain during the *fin de siècle*, in which women were subject to subordination.

Since these literary works are separated by the Atlantic Ocean, the perspective of Transatlantic studies helps one to understand similarities or disparities in these productions. In the essay "What Is Transatlantic Literary Studies?," Susan Manning and Andrew Taylor's main concern about these studies is that the disciplinary realm deals with comparisons of Transatlantic literary texts coming exclusively from America, Africa, and Europe—comparisons that in many cases are "trans- and post-nationalist political and cultural studies" (4). Nonetheless, here we will also explore texts from Spain and from Mexico, two countries that fit into the concept of Transatlantic comparisons. Heidi Slettedahl Macpherson suggests there is an opportunity to observe disparities among places, such as places divided by oceans, that have "the same critical framework of interest" (Slettedahl-Macpherson 6). For Slettedahl, Transatlantic studies bring to the forefront a multiplicity of connections in which there is not only space for contestation among texts and textualities but also a dimension of gender that adds important contributions to these conversations. In addition, Slettedahl Macpherson claims that in the "Atlantic space," there is a prominent place for women's literature.

Paul Giles contributes a great deal to Transatlantic studies and is well-known in this field. Giles points out the level of importance of "interactions" among authors in the Transatlantic context, which is not new. He includes questions regarding the substantial conversations between English and American literature (Giles 2). Although this author remarks on the comparison between the British and the United States literature as a principal point, the same principle can be used here between Spain's and Mexico's literature. Another annotation of Giles is that there is an inclination in many countries or continents to claim to have a homogenous cultural and literary production. Comparisons might be exclusively gathered from literary texts across the Atlantic and used as a comparative practice between these continents (Manning and Taylor 4-5). He also suggests that this idea should be evaluated to enhance the analysis of texts or other cultural products. This is related to the view of aesthetical disparities not only among Mexico, Spain, the United States, and Great Britain as countries of production but also among writers and texts. While these theoretical views are vital for this discussion, literary criticism is not less; therefore, it is reviewed in the next section.

Criticism

Javier Ordiz addresses different themes regarding the woman. Some of the topics that Ordiz studies are relevant for this chapter. These include the value of the woman in literary works and in the society at the end of the nineteenth century in Mexico. Additionally, he lectures about the symbolic relation between the main character's history and the nation's representations. Debra A. Castillo explores a new reading of Gamboa's novel from the perspective of contemporary feminism while analyzing the concept of female sexuality at the end of the nineteenth century. Additionally, Nancy LaGreca studies the main character of *La hija del bandido* by Barragán de Toscano. She notes how this character, María, the daughter of the bandit, distances herself from the scheme of the Angel of the House, a trend for women characters at the time. It is important to notice that the main character is still a progressive character, as LaGreca notices. Joyce Tolliver studies how Pardo Bazán's narrative depicts issues in women's sexuality, gender, or cultural expressions. In addition, she shows how the *femme fatale* scheme is present in this author's work. Susan Walter analyzes "Posesión" (1895) and "El rival" (1902). The works of these scholars make clear that the theme of the *femme fatale* is recurrent in Pardo Bazán's short stories. They will help to put in context the author of these short stories and her gender perspective. Barroso studies the evolution of Naturalism in different novels by Emilia Pardo Bazán. He addresses the conditions, space, time, hereditary traits, and relation of the characters with nature. His book illuminates how this author uses the Naturalism scheme. Maria Elana Ojea Fernández, in Narrativa feministas en los cuentos de la condesa de Pardo Bazán," presents how Pardo Bazán uses her concerns regarding violence against Spanish women at the turn of the century. It is important to emphasize that these works mentioned above help with different interpretations of the works of this author, but none of them address deviancies in the female characters from the Transatlantic point of view.

Regarding the trope of the *femme fatale* in the context of Louisiana, United States, two authors can be mentioned: Cyrille Arnavon and Jean Witherow. The first deals not only with the naturalistic aesthetics but also with the *femme fatale* scheme in Chopin's *The Awakening*. She compares Madame Bovary and Edna Pontellier as products of the same naturalistic crafting. Similarly, Witherow compares Flaubert's Naturalism with Chopin's narrative regarding the fate of the main characters. She finds a series of differences between the two authors. Nonetheless, these two scholars bring to light the conversation between the female characters of Edna Pontellier and Emma Bovary in regard to their suicide. When addressing the female character in the works of Thomas Hardy and Sarah Grand, the perspective of this feminism stands out. The scholar Ann Heilmann addresses in depth the New Woman's presence not only in Great Britain but also in the United States. Her works analyze different aspects of this early feminism. Her first work discusses extensively the social and political impact of the New Woman in England at the *fin de siècle*. In the book *Sex, Social Purity, and Sarah Grand*, she compiles a series of essays of Grand's that are the very basis of the New Woman perspective. Another important author in regard to British Literature is Sarah Grand. This chapter uses several of her essays that are relevant in the context of Hardy's and Grand's novels. Elaine Showalter gives a deep understanding of the New Woman in her interpretations of different texts from the movement. Another academic scholar of gender, the New Woman, and the late nineteenth century is Teresa Magnum. In her work, she addresses the novel *Ideala* and its engagement with the New Woman as an alternative discourse. Nonetheless, this chapter uses these major works on the New Woman not only with the British authors, but also with authors from Spain, Mexico, the United States. Finally, it is important to clarify that there are other studies mentioned below that are used to complement the analysis and discussion of the *femme fatale* structure in the novels of Gamboa, Barragán de Toscano, Pardo Bazán, Chopin, Grand, and Hardy.

Santa

In the Mexican novel *Santa*, the theme of the *femme fatale* is used and exploited to the maximum with all the aspects of the character of Radical Naturalism. Along with this particular aesthetic, there are also other, perhaps unique, cultural characteristics that might or might not converge with other texts from Spain. As in the novel of the Spanish author Eduardo López Bago *La prostituta* (1884), *Santa* lets us see the *femme fatale*. This theme can also be seen as a structure that presents a character, generally a young woman, who is addressed romantically and sexually by a man with whom she falls in love. Eventually, she falls into societal marginalization (e.g., in brothels and streets). She brings fatality and diseases to the brothel and herself. The events in the novels are embedded with an unfortunate fate for the men that surround these characters. In his novel, Gamboa uses aspects of the *femme fatale* trope with cultural nuances. For example, he uses rural landscapes to enhance the view of his main character, Santa.

The narrative line follows the aesthetics of Radical Naturalism, in which the role of the woman is constructed according to the idea of scientific observation and study of society, as Emile Zola suggests in his book *Experimental Novel* (1893). It is important to highlight that what Zola brings forth in his work is a series of empirical parameters of observation based on Claude Bernard's premises. Zola points out that "the novelist is equally an observer and an experimentalist" (8). He also highlights the difference between the idealist novelist and the naturalist novelist by focusing on a concrete object when he suggests that "idealistic refers to writers who cast aside observations...and base their works on the supernatural and the irrational" (26). While doing so, Zola educates writers who happen to be part of his project. In many cases, these writers happen to be doctors in medicine (e.g., Eduardo López Bago).

Gamboa's political entanglement was conservative and supported *porfirismo*, a government tendency of the conservative policy-making of Porfirio Díaz (Ordiz 14). During the *Porfirismo* the state tried to penetrate the countryside of modernity, represented by the military in the novel. It is important to highlight that the role of modernity in the Latin American context reflects diminished values of human beings, particularly women (Cánovas 93). Also, the traditional values, such as the principles of the Catholic Church that were kept in Chimalistac, became corrupt by the "Gendarmería Municipal de a Caballo," which interfered in the town's life as an element that opposed tradition (Ordiz 14-15). The contrast between the "rurales" and "La Gendarmería Municipal" makes clear a state of change, as the narrative points out: "No one in Chimalistac worried much about the change in military detachment... Instead of the rural ones, they [the government] sent the municipal gendarmery on horseback" (52-53).[1] It is a change in official authority, a new representation of the state, and a new representation of modernism. Furthermore, the occupancy of the space is an allegory of a modern patriarchal power invasion not only over the woman (Santa), but also over the old representation of authority. This view of modernity is negative.

This modernity is also expressed when the narrative points out how different their uniforms are: "... and the villains raised their shoulders; they will miss ... their leather chaps and jackets. The dress code is beyond their understanding of [their] European outfits" (53).[2] The dress code here embeds the modern representation, as during the nineteenth century, military uniforms were used as the nation's signifier. The novel underlines how modernization of the military displaces the Mexican traditional customs reflected in the dress code. In this respect, Michel Foucault suggests that "hierarchical observation" works in military contexts because it homogenizes, making the differences visible (Foucault, *Discipline & Punish* 176-177).

The plot develops through four stages in which the deterministic traits of a woman are represented in the main character, Santa. In stage one, the girl is

---

[1] "Nadie en Chimalistac se preocupó mayormente con el cambio de destacamento...en lugar de los rurales habían enviado los de la Gendarmería Municipal de a caballo" (52-53).
[2] "y los villanos se alzaron de hombros; echarían de menos ...las chaparreras y chaquetas de cuero de aquellos—Indumentaria mas al alcance de su compronsibilidad que los arreos a la europea de éstos" (53).

seduced by an officer of the Mexican army. In the second stage, she is expelled from her rural town by her own relatives. In the third stage, she becomes a prostitute. In the fourth stage, she intends to rehabilitate herself, but she falls sick and dies. In his essay "En los márgenes del Naturalismo," Javier Ordiz finds symbols in such a sequence, and he reads them as narrative functions of such a structure, suggesting that the novel moves along the following scaffold: "1) life in Paradise, 2) transgression, 3) expulsion, 4) expiation that occurs in the Purgatory of Mexico City, and 5) forgiveness and the redemption" (13).[3] The novel not only questions the reader's sexual and moral understanding but also suggests health and political implications of sexuality, among other representations (Rodríguez 404). The nation is a hetero-male construction, and the national project is based on the notion the nation is a feminine entity; thus, it has to be protected and included in the national imagination.

The story uses flashbacks in time with the narrator's intimate voice while connecting the reader and the main character in a personal way (Ordiz 9). It is a technique that introduces marginality and, thus, the setting and the secondary characters. This introduction is accomplished by disparate scenery in the first few pages of the novel, where the story presents the character of Pepa "Ah! The grotesque figure of Pepa … [,] her flesh out, curvy, the face and the neck, the big belly of a drinker, her weak breasts … oscillating grotesquely" (19).[4] The resonance of the binary system of normal/abnormal was not exclusive to medicine; it can be seen in other social and political contexts as well. By using this type of dialogue, Gamboa connects health, marginality, and morality to make social arguments. He also uses these connections to stress the depiction of a fallen woman to deliver his ideas about social and national issues. There is also the idea of the woman as a "social danger" when the character slowly dies of sickness connected with deviancy.

After the introduction, it is easy to see the main character's personal circumstances. Santa is from Chimalistac, a rural town, in which the plot highlights her origins as follows: "Her story! The vulgar story of poor girls who are born in the countryside and are raised in the open air between the breezes and flowers; an ignorant caste and strong in the care of the hearth" (39).[5] The retrospective allows this pastoral narrative not only to make comparisons to Santa's "natural" healthy origin but also to insert national symbolism in the

---

[3] "1) la vida en el Paraíso, 2) la transgresión, 3) la expulsión, 4) la expiación que lleva a cabo en el Purgatorio de la Ciudad de México; y 5) el perdón y la redención" (13).

[4] "¡Ah! La grotesca figura de Pepa… Sus carnes marchitas, exuberantes…la cara y el cuello, su enorme vientre de bebedora, sus lacios senos… oscilaban asquerosamente" (19).

[5] "¡Su historia! La historia vulgar de las muchachas pobres que nacen en el campo se crían al aire libre, entre brisas y flores; ignorantes castas y fuertes al cuidado de la tierra" (39).

characters and settings. Moreover, the depiction of the women as uneducated, innocent, naïve, and poor in the countryside at the mercy of the elements depicts the character of Santa as a *femme fatale*. In other words, the narrative voice judges the women morally, thereby undermining them. The narrator relegates their representation to a lower social class (Ordiz 9-10).

The narrator's male voice emphasizes the weakness of the women. Thus, they are an easy target for false promises, lies, and trickery. This observation converges with Toril Moi's findings, in which the arguments from the science related to sex and sexuality give women a low estimative value. Nonetheless, even as naïve, poor, uneducated, and mentally inferior in this context. Santa's women would need to maintain responsibility for their own actions (Ordiz 10). Santa believes the alférez Marcelino Beltrán's promises: "All in truth he had said to Santa; the innocent and candid words with which it is law that love begins" (55).[6] Santa, then, is caught in this dialogue between the true and the false, which leads her to be marginalized and fall to the bottom of society. She seems to be accountable for her sexual involvement with Beltrán.

She loses her control over her own desire(s), a particular trait of Radical Naturalism. Later, Santa's actions not only cause her to become a prostitute but also influence her involvement with deviant individuals such as la Gaditana. Women's predeterminism is also present in the story and stated by the misogynistic narrator: "The truth is that the women with their strong faculty for fakeness, never lose, never forget the gestures, words, or attitude that are in their favor" (169).[7] This excerpt highlights the idea of women as naturally dishonest and capable of any kind of malicious fabrications. Another aspect that can be mentioned as part of the *femme fatale* trope are mechanisms of control, in which family, society, or groups of friends can be considered control devices. In this novel, the family structure is the mechanism by which Santa is pushed out of a rural town as an outcast. These mechanisms of "normalizing judgment," which appear as the family, the workshop, and so on, create different punishments with the objective of control mechanisms (Foucault, *Discipline & Punish* 176-177). Santa's family consists of two brothers and a mother without the presence of the father. In addition, there is the alférez Marcelino Beltrán, who not only is a male figure but also plays the role of Don Juan. The male figure is part of the narrator's argument that highlights the women's determinism not only in the city but particularly in the rural zones of Mexico.

---

6 "Todo en verdad habíaselo dicho a Santa; las palabras inocentes y cándidas con las que es de ley que comiencen los amores" (55).

7 "Tan cierto es que las mujeres por su poderosa facultad de fingir no pierden jamás, ni jamás olvidan los gestos, palabras, o actitudes que las favorecen" (169).

Additionally, the narrator distances himself from the main character while at the same time underlining the character of Santa as an object. He complies with some of the parameters that Zola uses as part of the "experiment," as he recalls a quote from Claude Bernard: "The observer relates purely and simply to the phenomenon.... He listens to nature, and he writes under its dictation. But once the fact is ascertained and the phenomenon observed, an idea or hypothesis comes into his mind" (7). In other words, the writer not only sees and writes but also interprets all his/her subjects. Santa is in between two male figures and the mother. In the case of Santa, a combination of powers interacts to cause her fate as a fallen woman. Another factor is Santa's familial influences when she is expelled from her town:

> That one who is no longer a virgin, the bad daughter and the forgotten maiden ... [She] must be rejected ... She turned her face and only saw her mother in the arms of her brothers, her right hand raised as she was going to leave, like a solemn patriarchal group of vigilantes during biblical times. (65)[8]

The scene ends with a visual biblical reference, "los justicieros de tiempos bíblicos," which has resemblances to, and connotations of, "divine judgment" and "the expulsion of the Paradise" (Ordiz 12).

Gamboa exploits other aspects of the *femme fatale*, for instance, the Church's power, which appears when Santa cannot stay inside the Church's building. The state's power also manifests itself in many forms. One is the alférez Marcelino Beltrán as a symbol of the armed forces. Another is the medical doctors as an entity that regulates health. However, the narrator's views of these regulators are as a corrupted entity or office when they interact with Pepa: "Let them come in, stupid—Pepa commanded ... They are Health Department agents. ... And at the same time, they enjoy a certain character of being like the police ... whenever the professionals bribe them—they let major infractions go unnoticed" (138).[9] Gamboa makes us see corruption as another factor or agent that will affect Santa's fate. Corruption in this novel is presented as a force that promotes sickness on a regular basis. It is a social and political commentary in regard to public health. This combination of corruption and unhealthy

---

[8] "La que ha cesado de ser virgen, la mala hija y la doncella olvidadiza ... hay que rechazarla ...Volvió su rostro y solo contempló a su madre entre los brazos de sus hermanos, la diestra levantada como cuando mandara irse, en solemne grupo patriarcal de los justicieros de tiempos bíblicos" (65).

[9] "Déjalos que entren borrica — le indicó Pepa ... Son los agentes de Sanidad ...Y como a la vez disfrutan de cierto carácter de policías...cuando las profesionales les untan la mano ... — pasan inadvertidas las infracciones mayores" (138).

prostitutes represents a social threat, a socially dangerous stigma also carried by all the women in the novel. Health issues constitute another aspect of the *femme fatale*'s decadence and her depiction as a social or biological danger. This is a recurrent topic in the aesthetics of Naturalism. For example, Santa becomes an alcoholic, has pulmonary disease, and finally dies of cancer. This scheme is more emphatic in Radical Naturalism. In this case, the male voice of the narrator controls the spectacle, including its own judgmental commentaries about women, marginal women, and marginal places. The author crafts the character in a way that enhances the concept of women's inferiority from the perspective of the medical discourse.

The narrative of *Santa* is so incisive in its representation of the sick woman that this aspect of the novel becomes hyperbolic. Gamboa uses prostitution to dress this main character as a means of grasping the true possibilities of Santa. Furthermore, through medical knowledge, the novel unveils socioeconomic differences and the power of "bio-power," which is the capacity of science to make assertions toward society or toward the physical body. This patriarchal perspective happens when the narrator explains Santa's health problems:

> Santa's disease was so characteristic and so advanced that the physicians only needed one test to verify her sickness.... After the test, he called Hipólito to the terrace ... [,] and without waisting time, he told him the news:
> — she suffers from a terrible cancer that has no cure ... It is an incurable disease! ...
> [Hipólito] What you are saying is that without the surgery, the sick person will die soon?
> —Certainly, and soon, sir! ...What is the name of the surgery? Hipólito asked....
> Hysterectomy! ...
> And the confusing word stunned Hipólito, who found the word's structure and sound sinister. (283)[10]

---

[10] "La enfermedad de Santa era tan característica, tan avanzada se hallaba que el galeno tuvo de sobra con un solo examen ... Terminado el examen, llamó a Hipólito a la azotehuela ... y sin medias tintas disparó la nueva:
—Lo que padece la señora es un cáncer tremendo y sin, cura ... ¡Es un mal incurable! ...
¿Dice usted que sin operación es infalible y pronta la muerte de la enferma ...?
—infalible y pronta si señor! ... ¿Cómo se llama la operación? —preguntó Hipólito ...
¡Histerectomía! ... Y el enrevesado acabó de anonadarlo, encontraba enrevesada la estructura y siniestro el sonido" (283).

Hipólito's misunderstanding of the medical term points to the differences between the marginalized world and the society in which Santa lives. The omnipresent narrator emphasizes the doctor's words and lets the reader see how Hipólito interprets the term "histerectomía." In *La ciudad letrada* (1984), Angel Rama suggests that in Latin America after independence, the elite not only manipulated the national discourse in regard to the collective imagination but also manipulated knowledge. In other words, the elite controlled who could have access to education to control society and hold power. Hipólito's illiteracy shows his social position. Medicine at the time looked not only for a normal health state in individuals but also for the correction of what can be corrected and how this could be done (Foucault, *The Birth of the Clinic* 35). The resonance of the binary system of normal/abnormal is not exclusive to medicine. This can be seen in other social and political aspects as well.

Death is part of the *femme fatale* trope, as we can observe not only in *Santa* but also in López Bago's tetralogy, which includes his novel *La prostituta* (1884). *Santa* uses death to help craft a circular narrative. The novel compares Santa's voice at the beginning with her death and burial in the final pages: "Time continued rolling on; Santa had been buried months ago" (298).[11] This trait is common in naturalist novels, and the use of other strategies helps to construct the fate of the *femme fatale*. Then, *Santa* uses the structure of Naturalism in which a vulnerable "girl" who is at the mercy of nature is seduced by a man. Without options, she must follow the path of prostitution in which the sociopolitical situation of the characters and the settings unveil different social issues and political problems. Santa is not only sick but also can spread sickness to all the men with whom she is in contact. The appearance of sickness usually follows, and finally, it leads the female character to death. As in other novels such as those mentioned above, women in Radical Naturalism and many times in Naturalism fall and die because of their moral shortcomings.

Alternating between the Spanish author López Bago and the Mexican author Gamboa, the Galician author Pardo Bazán uses the *femme fatale* to highlight the unfairness of the patriarchal power. She debates the argument of women's determinism and brings forth the concept of the "New Woman." This term implies specific characteristics and the standing of women by the late nineteenth century. It is also intertwined with a social and political phenomenon in which women appear differently in many aspects of society. The New Woman's external constructions of this phenomenon many times used ambiguities in gender representation or images such as "non-female, unfeminine, and ultra-feminine" (Heilmann, *New Woman Fiction* 20). They also were used to spark a political and ideological presence in literature. The

---

[11] "El tiempo continuaba rodando; ya Santa llevaba meses de enterrada" (298).

novel could be used as a politically powerful tool. The New Woman, then, became a subversive element that had the main characteristic of disrupting social, literary, political, and artistical conventions of the *fin-de-siècle* (Heilmann, *New Woman Fiction* 1). This perspective as a phenomenon had a great deal of impact on literary production in Great Britain and in the United States (Bentley 141), though there were temporal disparities among these countries. In Spain and Mexico, the New Woman perspective had a different development, which was also nonlinear in terms of time. In other words, as Elaine Showalter suggests, "Unlike the odd woman, celibate, sexually repressed, and easily pitied or patronized as the flotsam and jetsam of the matrimonial tide, the sexually independent New Woman criticized society's insistence on marriage as woman's only option" (38) Other features of the New Woman such as dressing in pants, riding bicycles, and smoking cigarettes were easily noticed too. Images that appeared in different forms in literature referenced and represented many narratives of the time.

"Tío Terrones"

Pardo Bazán's narratives are essentially naturalistic (Tolliver 14), and the archetype of the *femme fatale* is frequently used not only in her novels but also in her short stories. Although Pardo Bazán's attitudes toward some aspects of the New Woman are ambiguous, she can be seen as a feminist of her era. Joyce Tolliver states, "Pardo Bazán's reference to the two humanist philosophers reflects a consciousness common to her feminist essays" (17).[12] The theme of the *femme fatale*, as Susan Walter points out in her essay "Images of the *Femme Fatale* in Two Short Stories by Emilia Pardo Bazán," is recurrent, at least in the cases that she analyses, "Posesión" (1895) and "El rival" (1902).

In "Tío Terrones" and in the novels *La piedra angular* and *La gota de sangre*, the structure of the *femme fatale* is not only present but also used as a device to critique the male gaze over women. The plot of this short story presents a rural family in which the father and the patriarchal representation is Crispín Terrones. He is an old man who lives with Petronila, Zoila, and other girls in a small town called Montonera. Early on in the story, the naturalistic aesthetic structure brings forth the woman who is prone to decline, a deviant in comparison with other women. Nonetheless, the narrative emphasizes the patriarchal power of Crispín Terrones through violence that appears when the narrator explains the situation:

---

[12] Tolliver's quotation relates to Fray Luis de León and Juan Luis Vives (see quotation on page 17).

In the town of Montonera, for about two months, there was no gossip
other than the exemplary punishment of Petronila, the daughter of
Uncle Crispín Terrones. Upon learning of the girl's slips [with a man],
her father inflicted a tremendous beating onto her with a stick of *taray*
—the one used to beat cloth when in fear of clothes moths —while doing
this, he solemnly cursed her as if he were exorcizing a madman, and
finally, after giving her a miserable bundle of belongings and thirty
pennies, he pushed her out his house while loudly saying: "—Go
wherever you want but you will never cross my door again." (1354)[13]

Yet early, the story presents the woman who brings disgrace to her house, which
resembles the *femme fatale* structure. It also brings to the fore paternal
punishment and the social attitudes toward these events. The events described
not only allow the reader to see such a structure but also define the fate of
Petronila. Moreover, this excerpt can be seen as a parallel, though not a perfect
one, to the novel of *Santa*. The two narratives suggest a clear pattern. First, a
woman/girl falls for a man. Second, the woman/girl is expelled from her
home/town. Third, the woman/girl is expelled into the outer world. Finally, she
becomes sick and dies, which is the fate of the main character, as in *Santa*.
Significantly, in "Tío Terrones," such a fate is not present.

Following the narrative line in "Tio Terrones," the reader notices that Petronila,
the woman who fails to uphold the family's traditions and dishonors family
values, does not fit into the naturalistic aesthetic scheme. On the contrary, she
becomes a prominent individual, at least in economic terms. It also omits the
suffering of the character, which is one of the main characteristics of Naturalism.
The narrator highlights how Petronila shows economic and social growth:

...but before the astonished town could be convinced of Aunt Hilaria's
insolent ostentatious expenditures ... [,] there was heated commentary
about the repair and expansion of the ruinous inn sparing no expense and
the acquisition of several plots of the most productive land. (1354-55)[14]

---

[13] "En el pueblo de Montonera, por espacio de dos meses, no se habló sino del ejemplar
castigo de Petronila, la hija del tío Crispín Terrones. Al saber el desliz de la muchacha, su
padre había empezado por aplicarle una tremenda paliza con la vara de taray –la de
apalear la capa por miedo a la polilla–, hecho lo cual, la maldijo solemnemente como
quien exorciza a un energúmeno y, al fin, después de entregarle un mezquino hatillo y
treinta reales, la sacó fuera de la casa, fulminando en alta voz esta sentencia: ... '–Vete a
donde quieras que mi puerta no has de atravesarla más en tu vida'" (1354).

[14] "...pero antes de que el pueblo atónito se convenciese del insolente boato que gastaba

Although the connection to Hilaria becomes important at the beginning of the story, the excerpt lets the reader see the proportions of the economic improvement of Petronila. The narrative reiterates Petronila's change of fate in her sister's voice when she recounts the rumors about her:

> a sister richer than the Bank of Spain! … She runs around all over the place, and yesterday at the pharmacy the doctor don Tiodoro explained … It seems that she was in Madrid and that she lives in a big house like a palace and doesn't need anything. She even has a car with two plump mares that not even the bishop has. (1355)[15]

The emphasis on Petronila's economic advances foregrounds the disassembly of the *femme fatale* structure and, therefore, a new fate for a woman character. Petronila does not decline into sickness or death. She brings prosperity to her hometown. Pardo Bazán's narrative, no doubt, depicts power and control through sex, sexuality, gender, cultural conceptions, and language. Pardo Bazán's short stories enhance not only women's virtues of independence, determination, and energy but also the situation of the abused woman. This writer used to write about violence against women in a periodical magazine, "La ilustración artística." In "Tío Terrones," Pardo Bazán lets the reader know her interest in regards to violence against women, particularly by men.

The change in the fate of Petronila helps to introduce the New Woman concept in this story, as it presents her as a successful and independent woman. The story accurately differentiates Petronila from marginal, biologically damaged, or mentally ill individuals. She does not show sickness of any kind, and there is no evidence of other types of deviancies in her. On the contrary, the story underlines certain values in Petronila. For instance, the narrative also focuses on her inner strength at the time she was expelled and beaten: "[She] silently lowered her head and went to the inn" (1354).[16] The story also unveils Petronila's noble heart, as she is thankful to Hilaria when Zoila tells tío Terrones: "All the Asian luxury of Aunt Hilaria, do you know where it comes from? I bet

---

la tía Hilaria … se comentasen acaloradamente las obras de reparación y ensanche emprendidas a todo coste en el ruinoso mesón, y la adquisición de varios terrenos de labradío de los más productivos" (1354-55).

[15] "una hermana más rica que el Banco de España! … Ta corre por todo el lugar, y ayer en la botica lo explicó el medico don Tiodoro … Paice que estála Petronila en Madri, y que vive en una casa grande a mo de palacio, y por no faltarle cosa alguna, hasta coche lleva con dos yeguas rollizas que ni las mulas del señor obispo" (1355).

[16] "silenciosamente bajó la cabeza y se dirigió al mesón" (1354).

you don't. It comes from Petronila!" (1355).[17] Here, the text does not leave space for any doubts about Petronila's noble personality. The storyline makes it difficult for its audience to make negative assumptions about her way of living. It does not give the reader any evidence that could lead to negative assumptions.

The moral values are inverted. At the beginning, the text highlights Petronila's "desliz" (slip), which is the main moral issue. Alternatively, Tío Terrones and his daughter "Zoila" maintain hypocritical positions throughout toward the family's moral values. The economic dependency of men in the late nineteenth century is marked as one of tío Terrones' responses to Petronila's "desliz" and the thirty *reales* are the representation of such dependency. This leads her to this submissive position that gives no other way to respond to this paradigm. She cannot do anything but lower her head and nod.

Pardo Bazán highlights in Zoila and her father the decadence of their societal values whenever they are interested in Petronila's assets, as in the dialogue between the two:

> All the Asiatic luxuries that Aunt Hilaria has, do you know where they come from? ... [They] come from Petronila. ... Now what do you have to say about that? Let's see. —And what do you want to me say? —replied the sullen crestfallen man with a wrinkled brow and with his head lowered. (1355)[18]

While she inquires about Pertronila's economic position, Zoila acts as a moral conscience that appears in the resentful tone toward her father, Crispín.

In previous dialogue, Zoila and her father reveal other moral positions such as pride, greed, and, most of all, the question of the acquisition of money when Zoila points out:

> —What do I want? Come on, come on! It is not a sin against God that the strangers might take all [the money] but the blood relatives do not even know that we have a sister richer that the Bank of Spain. ...
> —Let them be! grumbled Uncle Terrones roughly, cheerless and frowning— the ill-gotten money will be taken advantage by the ones using it to eat! ...

---

[17] "Tos los lujos asiáticos de la tía Hilaria ¿sabe usté de ónde alen? ¿A que no? ¡De la Petronila" (1355).

[18] "Tos los lujos asiáticos de la tía Hilaria, ¿sabe usté de ónde salen? ...De la Petronila... ¿y ahora qué ice usté deso, amos a ver? ... —Y ¿qué quieres que yo te diga? —respondió el paleto hosco y cabizbajo. Con una arruga profunda en la frente y dejando arrastrar la mirada por el suelo" (1355).

—And how do you know if it is wrongly earned? (1355)[19]

Zoila not only questions Crispín's perspective of Petronila and her money but also enables the reader to disregard the negative assumptions about Petronila's sexual behavior. In this way, Pardo Bazán intersects the schema of Naturalism and its aesthetics to transform the negative model of a *femme fatale* into a New Woman type of character.

The narrator, then, intervenes to explain the reasons for Zoila and Crispín's interest in Petronila's money, as the story continues: "[Then] they said nothing, father and daughter, but without avid glances, their folded foreheads, their little eyes in which greed gleamed involuntarily, they expressed themselves with ample eloquence. Zoila was the first one who resolved to formulate the dark desire of her will" (1355).[20] Tío Terrones' greed appears as a counterpoint to moral values. In other words, this altercation presents a double standard and the reverse of Christian Catholic values. Overall, the story presents the family as a vigilant apparatus similar to "panopticism." The panopticon can be used as a social device to police members of society. In the case of "Tío Terrones," the father functions as a policing device.

Crispín's meditations about his role in Petronila's life guide us to see how he changes his moral position. He thinks of his daughter's problem back when he had a decisive role in affecting Petronila's future by condemning her. He also thinks that at the time of these events, he felt such actions were especially romantic, like in the old Spanish way. Furthermore, the narrator emphasizes the contrasts between Crispín Terrones's meditative thoughts and his words when he states, "But the honor? Bah! Who cares about the honor of a poor man? How many times does deceitful money take the guise of honor!" (1355).[21] This dialogue lets us see the patriarchal power in practice. Nonetheless, the dialogues between Tío Terrones and Zoila raise intriguing questions about Petronila's uses of her sexuality while implying that she is a prostitute. As mentioned above, these depictions are one of the primary traits of the New Woman perspective. Elaine Showalter presents this aspect of the New Woman,

---

[19] "—¿Qué quiero? ¡Anda, anda! ¡Que es un pecao contra Dios que se lo lleven a los extraños y los parientes por la sangre no sepamos siquiá que tenemos una hermana más rica que el Banco España! ... ¡Allá ellas! —refunfuñó el tío Terrones ásperamente, sombrío y ceñudo— ¡Lo mal ganao, que le aproveche a quien lo come! ... ¿Y usté qué sabe si es mal ganao?" (1355).

[20] "Callaron padre e hija, pero sin miradas ávidas, sus plegadas frentes, sus ojillos, en que relucía involuntariamente la codicia, se expresaron con sobrada elocuencia. Zoila fue la primera que se resolvió a formular el oscuro anhelo de su voluntad" (1355).

[21] "Pero ¿La honra? ¡Bah! ¿A quién le importa la honra de un pobre? ¡Cuántas veces el pícaro dinero toma figura de honor!" (1355).

arguing that sexual independence was a form of social criticism, counterpointing the regular role of marriage as the only option for women at the beginning of the twentieth century.

In the last scene, Crispín Terrones tells Zoila about his decision to write a note to Petronila:

> frowning with sudden energy and getting up as if he was ending the discussion, he said in the most decisive and dry way, full of dignity and intransigence:
> —The ink with which I write to that slut, does not yet exist and it will not be made, woman. (1355)[22]

Suddenly, Crispín Terrones begins feeling like a powerful patriarchal father again while the narrator describes how he acts. This end reveals that he would nonetheless maintain his patriarchal arrogant inflexibility and his lack of education. The character's projecting image and his inner thoughts in dialogue underline hypocrisy. This excerpt ends with these sentences from Crispín Terrones:

> [Tío] Terrones stopped for a moment and muttered without any change in tone:
> —Now, if you want to write ... [,] daughter, I will not say no or do anything, but you, you are different. That's why you went to school, and you make those letters so rounded that it looks as if you only studied to work as a calligrapher! (1355)[23]

This dialogue reveals how Crispín Terrones is hiding his intentions and his patriarchal posture. In other words, the main character will let his daughter write the note, without telling her. The work of Pardo Bazán is a social critique in which the characters are under patriarchal dominance. It is important to highlight that the views of the series of women are dominated by an old, weak, and hypocritical man who has power over them put in place by the patriarchal society. Embedded in this situation is Petronila, an imagined deviant who goes

---

[22] "frunciendo las cejas con repentina energía levantándose como para cortar la discusión, exclamó del modo más rotundo y seco, lleno de dignidad e intransigencia:
—La tinta con que yo le escriba a esa pindonga, no sa fabricao ni sa de fabricar, mujer" (1355).

[23] "Terrones se detuvo un momento y masculló sin transición de tono:
—Ahora si tú quiés escribir ... Hija, no digo ... Tú es otra cosa. Pa eso has io a la escuela y haces ese letruz tan redondo que ¡no paice sino que estudiabas el oficio de mimorialista!" (1355).

outside the norm to survive. Petronila's character is crafted in the Naturalism aesthetics or *femme fatale* trope, but it does not follow all the schematics. She is a successful individual; after being left to her own fate, she overcomes her position by making money and returning to the old town. Petronila cannot be framed by the prostitution scheme because there is no indication of it in the text. In fact, the narrative prevents such thought when Zoila asks her father, "And how do you know if it is wrongly earned?" (1355).[24] The truth is that no one knows where Petronila's money comes from. At the same time, the story warns readers not to believe Crispín Terrones. In fact, this character is a violent and uneducated man who beats his own daughter because of rumors. Here, the reader can see another perspective of the deviant woman and a view of women in general at the *fin de siècle*. Petronila, in this context, is a victim of her own father. It is important to mention that, though marriage was a way out of economic dependency, this short story presents a character who succeeds in both marriage and business. These perceptions were not exclusive to Spain. Similar ideas existed in Mexico by the end of the nineteenth century.

La hija del bandido

La hija del bandido depicts an active female character in a banditry environment from the Mexican colonial past. The story shows her being raised by her father, Vicente Colombo, who is a bandit. She is not aware of her father's banditry. She knows all her father's subordinates. This is a nonlinear story of María, a main character at the age at which girls are presented to society known in Mexico as *quinceañera* (LaGreca 60-63). Although she lives in this environment, she is still a sweet and beautiful young woman with virtues. María is brave, honest, and compassionate. These virtues are highlighted throughout the narrative. One example is when she finds her grandfather: "The girl made an effort to look cheerful" (186).[25] Another is when she needs to be honest with Rafael: We are in a field, said María, in which one needs to be honest" (186).[26] Both instances, though not the only ones, enhance María's virtues. She gains more presence in the structures of the story's timeline before the Mexican independence in rural Mexico. These aspects help to frame the view of a complex and ambitious woman/girl who, according to her circumstances, must deal with banditry. Although, to some extent, her father maintains total control of María, including her innocence and memories, she succeeds in overcoming the state of submission. Such representation brings up a discussion of the role of gender in these places. The male roles vary across the

---

[24] "¿Y usté qué sabe so es mal ganao?" (1355).
[25] "La joven hizo un esfuerzo para aparecer alegre" (186).
[26] "Tocamos un terreno —dijo María, en que es preciso ser franca" (186).

novel with different degrees of patriarchal representations. Vicente Colombo acts not only as the father but also as the authority of the state. Nonetheless, Colombo desires to leave banditry to become a regular citizen.

Colombo's presence appears in a dialogue with another person who was kidnaped and to whose identity he planned to steal in order to become a regular citizen when he states:

> — "Now then, —he said desperately: Kill me!
> Tear me into pieces now that I am under you power ...
> —I have no need to waste my time for a paper signed by that hand or Cecilia. You choose." (14)[27]

Colombo is a despicable bandit who seems to know his role well. Nonetheless, he loves María and wants to clear his name as he says, "If I could give my daughter a clear name tomorrow, a name that would protect her" (11).[28] His power is not only extended to the hideout domain but also covers the rural land and the towns in the surrounding areas, as one can infer from the dialogue with his captive, a relative of María's mother and her kidnapper:

> Take everything out of here! ... But do not harm my daughter ... [-says María's grandfather]
> —Your daughter will live from now on like a queen, —says one of Colombo's bandits— From that moment, to the day you were born, I cannot account for my deeds ... [I am so] unhappy! —I exclaimed in a fit of pity —the infamous bandit Vicente
> Colombo will sentence you to death in this very prison, as he did with me! (24-25)[29]

The conversation enhances the perception of the women as objects of the father's love and as objects of interchangeable value. In both cases, the idealization of the daughter is relevant and acts in the plot as an element

---

[27] " —Pues bien, — exclamó el preso con deseperación: ¡matadme!
¡hacedme pedazos, ya que estoy en vuestro poder ...
—No tengo necesidad de perder el tiempo: por un papel firmando por esa mano; o Cecilia. Escogéd" (14).
[28] "si yo pudiese mañana dar a mi hija un nombre limpio que la protegiera" (11).
[29] "—¡Lleváos todo que hay aquí! ... pero no hagáis mal a mi hija ....
—Vuestra hija va a vivir desde hoy como una reina, —dijo uno de ellos—
Desde ese momento, hasta el día que naciste, no puedo dar cuenta de mis ideas... —
—¡Desdichada! —exclamo en un arranque de lástima—, el bandido, el infame Vicente Colombo, te sentenciará a morir en esta prisión como me ha sentenciado a mí!" (24-25).

inherited from Romanticism. Also, the vision of the woman is the representation of the nation. These views present the system that Tamar Mayer sees as the interactions between gender and nation. Mayer unveils in the nineteenth-century context and suggests the nation represents a woman whom men need to defend. In this sense, María differs from Radical Naturalism's representation and more greatly resembles the New Woman's. A citation of Sor Juana Inés de la Cruz becomes relevant to highlight men's patriarchal status and privilege (LaGreca 76), as María points out: "All men are just like that— ... you judge, detest, and disregard without examining" (171).[30] The epilogue presents María as a nun and is a representation that separates the character from society and, more importantly, from men. This enhances not only María's character as the ideal woman and heroine but also her Catholicism, which is an important part of the signifier of Mexican identity. Similarly, as other references in the novel suggest, the combination of Catholic Mexican identity does not interfere with the embodiment of a woman as a strong subject, counterpointing the patterns of social, medical, and psychological views of the women at the time, as argued by Toril Moi. In other words, Barragán de Toscano brings forth a good example of women's resistance to patriarchal power.

The novel reflects an unstable society redeemed by a woman, which was not a common depiction in Mexico at the time of the novel (Zalduondo xxi). As Nancy LaGreca points out about the female character, "Barragán's narrative is significant as an early feminist work not only because it features a dynamic female character, but also because it employs in its narrative strategy dominant (masculine) culture's fissures" (77). Furthermore, the main character in Barragán's novel is not diluted like Gamboa's main character, Santa. On the contrary, María becomes more solid when she is related to the Mexican national identity through Catholicism. Here, Barragán de Toscano recalls Mexican Romanticism, like Altamirano's *Clemencia* (1869), with an identity that also comes back to the woman figure as pure like the nation but strong. The character of María takes distance from Gamboa's novel, in which the character of Santa is defeated by all aspects of life. The character of María is a paradox because she belongs to her father's band of outlaws, but she becomes a heroine when she destroys the troop. She does not appear as a victim. Nonetheless, in the Mexican context, the novel suggests that Barragán de Toscano can parallel the New Woman perspectives. This novel presents a different type of woman who frees not only herself but also the town and her land from banditry. This trait is also evident in Pardo Bazán's *La piedra angular* [*The Cornerstone*]. This novel also raises questions about the protagonist as a victim or a murderer. The

---

[30] "Así sois los hombres todos— ... juzgáis, aborrecéis, y despreciáis sin examinar" (171).

narrative presents different aspects of Spanish society. It focuses on changes to emphasize the view of the woman.

La piedra angular

La piedra angular presents different aspects of crime in the countryside of Marimedina. The first stage is related to Doctor Moragas. His socioeconomic position as a medical doctor allows him to get involved in political discussions against the death penalty. The plot also guides the reader to learn of Juan Rojo, the town's executioner, who has a disruptive relationship with society. Finally, the reader is directed toward a crime in which a passive character is referred to in the third person. The crime itself consists of a man's assassination in which his wife and his brother are supposedly involved.

Juan Rojo, the executioner, is related to the state's power to kill criminals, which causes tensions within society and affects his son, Telmo. Moragas has a two-year-old girl, Nené, whom he wants to raise as naturally as possible. These stories go hand in hand. While Moragas lives his life as a doctor, Juan Rojo continues as the executioner and sees himself as a public servant. Moragas is interested not only in the politics of the death penalty but also in those of any event as the narrator describes:

> A natural writing tendency exists in every man, even in the least literate … [It is] what [we] can called the *natural novelist*, capable of plotting in a few minutes more than thirty complicated bizarre arguments. Moragas possessed this ability to a high degree …[,] but after he spoke with the judge, his fantasy was working on the topic of crime and the enigma therein. (299)[31]

The narrative gives a brief ironic description of the naturalist writer. In "La cuestión palpitante," Pardo Bazán critiques several authors of Naturalism, including Emile Zola. For Pardo Bazán, Zola, as a "chief of Naturalism," lacks simplicity and naturalness (Pardo Bazán 628). In this novel, something similar happens. The narrator portrays the main character as a nosy person. There are also other instances in which the narrator implies that Moragas likes to make fantasies. For example, in Moragas' soliloquy, when he is helping Juan Rojo's son, he states, "You have reached the limit of this crazy charity.… If you want to become interested in something extraordinary and rare, congratulate yourself,

---

[31] "Existe en todo hombre, en el menos literato … lo que puede llamarse un *novelista natural*, capaz de urdir en pocos minutos treinta argumentos complicados y estrambóticos. Moragas poseía en alto grado esta facultad … pero después de hablar con el juez su fantasía trabajaba sobre el tema del crimen y del enigma probable que el encerraba" (299).

and pay attention to the parricide that you saw occur today" (305).[32] In other words, the narrative line depicts Moragas as a naturalist writer who fantasizes about parricide as an object of study —it was very common for naturalist writers to be doctors in medicine. This work suggests ethical flaws in this character, who has a great deal of skill in making quick arguments and a vivid imagination.

In the novel, men's presence is overwhelming, whereas women's presence is limited. Female characters are hardly active, while some women appear in a few dialogues. Although in a passive role, the character of the criminal woman gains her presence through her lack of physical presence. She appears in most cases in the third person. Another important aspect of these women is the role of the mother. Throughout the narrative, the mother is absent, and her absence is noticeable only through the children's characters. For example, Telmo is presented as nostalgically missing his mother. He also roams the streets at will. Nené's mother has died, and she is alone with her father, who wants to educate her in a particular way: "the doctor took care of her as one would take care of a mother...physiologically" (297).[33] She will be raised through science in an educational program led by her father, one in which natural contact and freedom are important for her development.

Nonetheless, part of the main point of the novel is the crime of a woman. A man has been killed, and his wife has been indicted as the assassin with the involvement of the dead man's brother. The reader meets this woman when the police catch her in the countryside near town. Apart from the event, the narrator makes his own rash conclusion about the case and sketches the woman. This description comes earlier to portray her:

[She] was a little thin in the face and the body. She had delicate features and regular lines in the contour of her breast, high and modest, over a plain waist. The hair, very black and separated on both sides over the temples with two braids hanging on the back. These contributed to her expression and presented a modest almost mystical appearance. (300)[34]

---

[32] "Ya has llegado al límite extremo de la chifladura benéfica.... Si quieres interesarte en algo raro y estupendo, interésate enhorabuena por la parricida a quien viste pasar hoy" (305).

[33] "el doctor la cuidaba como la cuidaría una madre ... fisióloga" (297).

[34] "...menudita de cara y cuerpo, de facciones delicadas y regulares de líneas en el contorno del seno, alto y pudoroso, sobre un talle plano. El pelo, muy negro y partido a ambos lados sobre las sienes y colgando atrás dos trenzas, contribuía a presentarle expresión y aspecto de recato casi místico" (300).

It is important to highlight that the description is nothing special. It is merely a description of a woman.

Also, the story presents interpretations of the legislation with regard to murder from Moragas' and other male characters' points of view. Among other instances involving the female character, her parricide causes Moragas to start to feel physical attraction toward her: "[She] would leave him deeply thoughtful, that girl so fragile, apparently so sweet, taken to jail … the woman's appearance had sparked in him a curiosity so similar to interest" (300).[35] This scenery not only evokes Moragas' erotic attraction toward this woman but also suggests a patriarchal guise. Nineteenth-century female writers used reversed elements to point out a return to primitivism (Dijkstra 65). In this sense, a Doctor of Medicine lets loose his primitive inner desires.

The lawyers, the judge, Moragas, and other characters discuss legalities in the case of the murder by a woman and by her male accomplice. This scenario sparks an important comment from the judge, who tries to describe the woman in terms of how she looks as he states:

> —And [that] woman who goes to prison, what kind of role does she play in this? …
> —A big one! Have you seen her?
> So…that…doesn't she look like a good woman? So, either I'm lying to myself…or she is the executer … or, at least co-executer … [,]
> the wife of the dead man … [,] better said, the widow of the murdered —
> Priego added with enthusiasm, while starting to bite the little tart. (301)[36]

The judge's tone and description indicate a negative perception of this woman (the *parricida*). Such judgmental expressions need explanation when he suggests what she "looks like" in an effort to enhance negative traits or physiognomies of the woman. These assertions by the judge represent ideas of determinism, social Darwinism, and Lombrosian measurements, which were embedded into the judicial system. The figure of the judge is also connected with impartiality, a trait

---

[35] "Le dejara profundamente pensativo aquella muchacha tan débil, tan dulce en apariencia llevada a la cárcel … el aspecto de la mujer le había despertado curiosidad parecidísima al interés" (300).

[36] "—Y mujer que va presa ¿qué papel juega en todo ello?…
—¡Una friolera! ¿la ha visto usted?
tan … así … que parece que no rompe un plato? Pues, o mucho me engaño … [,]
o es autora material … [,] o, por lo menos coautora … la mujer del muerto … [,] mejor dicho, la viuda del interfecto —añadió Priego festivamente empezando a mascullar un pastelillo" (301).

that every judge should have. The story criticizes the institution of justice in Spain and the scientific perspectives that guide it.

Nonetheless, Moragas adds more discursive statements on the vision of women from a medical perspective in his soliloquy:

> Moraguitas ... [,]now you have reached the extreme limit of the crazy charity ... If you want to have an interest in something weird and great, get interested in the parricide that is happening on the road now. [37] [She] can be a criminal, and let's admit it. Of course, she is but a criminal in an act of passion. ... At the moment of committing the crime, without doubt she acted on an irresistible impulse, caring neither about the other side of the pit that she would jump over nor about atonement for the outrageous death. ... That woman, Moraguitas, is a sick woman like any other of the ones who you treat. ... There is the explanation and the justification of the pity. (305)[38]

This monologue by Moragas not only reiterates his erotic interest in this woman but also adds the idea of predeterminism—a view that was in vogue in the late nineteenth century. It also gives prominence to the idea that a woman needs to be guided by a man because she lacks control over her own actions (Dijkstra 65).

There are other similar commentaries from the perspectives of lawyers, judges, and doctors on this passive female character. However, commentaries from the character of her accomplice are not present. Also, she is charged without any proof (at least there are no references to it in the text). Tsuchiya suggests that being a woman in Spain in the late nineteenth century was similar to being a deviant individual. In this town, everyone has an opinion about the crime or about its participants, though the expressions of such opinions come from male characters. Some of them think that she might have been a victim of her husband. Others, on the contrary, think that she has had an affair with her brother-in-law. The medical view repeats the idea, in vogue at the time, of the

---

[37] Moraguitas is a warm diminutive expression, in this case used by the main character to refer to himself.

[38] "Moraguitas ... Ya has llegado al limite extremo de la chifladura benéfica ... si quieres interesarte por algo raro y estupendo, interésate enhorabuena por la parricida a la carretera. ¡Esa podrá ser una criminal, y admitamos desde luego, que lo es; pero criminal en caliente ... [,] criminal pasional, que al delinquir obró sin duda, por irresistible impulso, sin importarle que al otro lado del foso que iba a saltar estuviese la expiación de una muerte afrentosa ... [,] esa mujer, Moraguitas es una enferma como otra cualquiera de las que asistes. ... Ahí se explica y se justifica la compassion" (305).

physical and psychological inferiority of women. At the time, the scientific approach toward men and women created the need for the feminist movement to make distinctions between social norms and biological differences (Moi 15). In other words, there was a need for a new view of these particular texts so that the ideology that they carry will be challenged. Another important aspect of the novel is that once the crime is mentioned, characters such as Nené or Telmo disappear from the events. However, the male presence is constant all the time from beginning to end. Men dominate all spaces and dialogues. Interventions by female characters are scarce. Such a strong male presence is accompanied by wrong decisions, erratic thoughts, and violence. Telmo, for example, ends up unconscious by a rock while he is attacked by other adolescents. There is an allegorical view of the mother in the "Epilogo" when María Roldán, Telmo's mother appears in front of Juan Rojo in a dialogic representation:

> María and Telmo; not the Telmo already grown up, but the one as he was in his mother's arms; [Juan] saw his little hands … that were reaching out … and were fumbling for the mother's breast. … Mother and child were, thus, full of intimacy, [full] of communicative sweetness, they laughed, they flattered themselves; but as Juan Rojo approached, the group dissolved; the mother threw the baby far away and fled … quickly. (348)[39]

This vision of Juan Rojo makes a reference not only to the virginal view of the mother but also to the abandonment of the child in her hands, which is stated as "throwing the baby far away." This is a dysfunctional society in which the dominance of men is always present in all spaces.

The "cornerstone" is an allegorical name used in the novel to refer to the death penalty, which was thought to keep society united. Looking at this disorganized society and the constant perception of the absence of women in all social spheres leads to the thought that the cornerstone, the column of a better society, is the strong presence of women. In other words, the cornerstone of a better society is not the death penalty but rather women. In this sense, Emilia Pardo Bazán makes a social and literary critique of the role women play in society and contests the patriarchal discourse. The perception of women through men's eyes allows the construction of the "deviant woman." This is another way to present women in patriarchy, and it is not only evident in the novel but also part of the novel's

---

[39] "María y Telmo; pero no a Telmo ya crecido, sino tal cual era en brazos de su madre; vio sus manitas … que salían … y buscaban a tientas el seno maternal. … Madre y crio así apretados llenos de intimidad, de dulzura comunicativa, se reían, se halagaban; pero al acercarse Juan Rojo deshacíase el grupo; la madre arrojaba al a la criatura lejos, muy lejos y salía huyendo … rápidamente" (348).

purpose. It is important to highlight that Pardo Bazán in *La cuestion palpitante* profoundly studies Naturalism, and she, no doubt, uses Naturalistic techniques in her works. Nonetheless, the Naturalism aesthetic in her narratives lacks determinism ("vacio de determinismo") (Barroso 30). Moreover, the novel's Radical Naturalism, or even Naturalism alone, brings forth the inner thoughts and views of its characters. In this sense, the novel becomes a sort of meta-naturalistic aesthetic narrative while, at the same time, it makes the reader a spectator of Radical Naturalism. In other words, the novel's naturalistic structure is used to counterpoint Naturalism itself.

Pardo Bazán was highly criticized during her time, in particular, because of the use of this literary style. The male dominance in literary criticism led to harsh public commentaries on her works. A critique from Leopoldo Alas (Clarín) can be highlighted, in which he suggested that Pardo Bazán's works and themes were limited and that her Naturalism style lacked the knowledge the world needed. Alas adds that the lack of knowledge was caused because she had no access to a "certain kind of woman" (Tolliver 23), access that seems to be a requirement for Naturalism narratives. Other writers, such as Bobadilla, Pereda, Menéndez, and Pelayo, united their voices with Clarín in criticism of Pardo Bazán's works (Tolliver 21).

These aesthetics in Pardo Bazán's *La piedra angular* do not share the *femme fatale* trope of the works of López Bago and Gamboa. The aesthetics are also distinct from Barragán de Toscano and, to some extent, from her own character, Petronila, in "Tio Terrones." However, at the end of the novel, the female character (the one who commits the parricide) disappears from the scope of the narrative as it shifts its focus to Juan Rojo, though there is no evidence of her death. Moreover, the novel does not indicate or suggest sickness or other predetermined "deviancies" in any woman, whereas it does present the drinking problem through Juan Rojo, who is linked with alcohol.

Aspects of the New Woman in the novel are not well marked, though it is important to mention Juan Rojo's spouse, María Telmo's mother, raises questions about her own family life. This story presents María Roldán as a passive character who is absent from her role of mother and spouse. We find her only in remembrances of Telmo and Juan Rojo, as well as the narrator's voice. Nonetheless, the character leaves the house because of Juan Rojo's social rejection:

> As for the rest, all the neighborhoods knew that María was resolved to take advantage of any confusion and run away "with the first man who showed up ..." She already said this many times... "And if I do not find

another desperate one, I do not care; I will take care of myself. There is
always the house of Nueve Tejas"[40]...
—As a good woman I have no match, not even the queen—... But if God
and the Virgin Mary where to punish me with my husband taking such
a job, with faith in Colasa, I would go with the soldiers in the barracks.
(295)[41]

María's determination to leave, empower herself, and govern herself, leading to
her independence, can be seen as one characteristic of the New Woman. Under
this view, as mentioned above, women's independence is a very important
aspect. This perspective relates not only to difficulties in a troubled marriage
but also to sexual scandals and empowerment of the woman's own sexuality
(Showalter 39). However, the New Woman movement not only resonated in
Spain, as we see in Pardo Bazán's novel, but it was also widely known much
earlier in the United States and in England.

The Awakening

In the Southern United States, in Louisiana, Chopin advances the idea of the
awakening from the marriage of the main character, Edna Pontellier. The novel
deals with the idea of a troublesome marriage and her awakening from it, as
much of early twentieth-century criticism suggests (Pollard 179). In this
narrative, while Edna is going through the process of "awakening," the story
crafts the fate of the character through the frame of Naturalism aesthetics, in
which she deteriorates and finally disappears in death. Although the work uses
these techniques, it unveils, at the same time, a counterargument as in the New
Woman. Nonetheless, the main character is crafted through the idea of
deviance. In the midst of this troublesome marriage, we find that part of Edna's
"awakening" has to do with having a counter-position to her husband and
society. Early in the work, we see the idea of the woman's appearance from the
husband's perspective as he points out the following: "You are burnt beyond
recognition,' he added, looking at his wife as one looks at a valuable piece of
personal property ..." (4). The tone and the narrator's view of Edna's husband's
attitude towards her bring forth not only the idea of an authoritarian posture in

---

[40] The house of Nueve Tejas is a reference to a brothel. She suggests that as the last resort
she will not hesitate to go and live in a brothel.

[41] "Por lo demás, todo el barrio sabía que María estaba resuelta a tomar el tole 'con el
primero que se presentara ...' Se lo había dejado decir muchas veces ... 'Y si no encuentro
un desesperado, lo mismo da; ya me gobernaré. No faltan esas casas de las Nueve Tejas' ...
—A mujer de bien no me gana ni la reina— ... Pero si Dios y la Virgen me castigasen con
tomar el marido mío semejante oficio, a fe de Colasa que me iba con los soldados del
cuartel" (295).

Mr. Pontellier but also the idea of a valuable object in Edna. From this perspective, the novel constructs its dialogue between Naturalism and the idea of awakening, which mimics the New Woman reactionary counter-discourse. Sarah Grand sees problems with marriage when the men have too much power when she states that "the man is dragged down enough; but he, by the customs of society, can escape to a large extent from the dead weight of his self-inflicted destiny ... To the woman, as always, society, having been ordered by a man, has not been quite so kind" (119). Grand's criticism was widely known at the time of *The Awakening*. It was discussed not just in England but also in the United States, a dynamic that is also a back and forth between the literary works on both sides of the Atlantic Ocean.

Edna gives an unfamiliar answer to her husband, in which she makes clear her position in not obeying. The narrator describes Edna resting in the hammock and enjoying the night. She suddenly is interrupted by her husband, who asks:

> "What are you doing out here, Edna? I thought I should find you in bed," said her husband, when he discovered her lying there....
> "Are you asleep?" he asked, bending down close to look at her.
> "No." Her eyes gleamed bright and intense, with no sleepy shadows, as they looked into his. ...
> "Edna!" called Mr. Pontellier ...
> "Don't wait for me," she answered. ...
> "You will be cold out there," he said. ...
> "It isn't cold; I have my shawl." ...
> She heard him moving about the room; every sound indicating impatience....
> "Edna dear, are you coming soon?" ...
> "No; I am going to stay out here." ...
> "Léonce, go to bed," she said. "I mean to stay out here. I don't wish to go in, and I don't intend to. Don't speak to me like that again; I shall not answer you." (30-31)

Part of "the awakening" starts at this point in the novel. Edna claims space, governance, and respect from her husband, a situation that develops further in time. The narrator then introduces the sensation of being awake when she points out: "Edna began to feel like one who awakens gradually out of a dream, a delicious, grotesque, impossible dream, to feel the realities pressing into her soul" (31). The "impossible dream" and the feeling of reality are part of her sensation of having her own governance and free will. Furthermore, such a "new" situation also causes the lowering of her husband's authoritarian expression, which, in the end, fades out. These traits are also found in other Chopin's and Sara Grand's narratives, such as novels and short stories.

The fact that Edna Pontellier becomes involved sexually with another man leads the reader to see her as a potential deviant who ends up as a *femme fatale*. This type of role can be understood because she is seen as mentally ill, as expressed and declared by their family's doctor. In this sense, the character starts to deteriorate, ultimately leading toward a fatal ending, as in *Madame Bovary* (1856). Nonetheless, this narrative treatment comes from the structure of the *femme fatale*, as in Gamboa or López Bago. While she overcomes her husband's authority and reduces his power to a minimum, she does not do the same with her father. In *Santa*, for example, the main character is active throughout the entire narrative. She also, like Edna, seems to struggle with mental illness, but overall, her health issues are related to her body. Gamboa's narrative line leads one to see how Santa's life becomes the cause of her death. This line of events does not converge with Edna's death because the cause of her suicide is unclear. Both characters die from different causes. While Santa is physically ill, Edna Pontellier suffers more from social separation and psychological trauma.

The last scene is vital from the perspective of Naturalism and from the New Woman. This scene can be a representation of the last break, where the sea is no longer a barrier, as the scene presents her last moments: "She looked into the distance, and the old terror flamed up for an instant, then sank again. Edna heard her father's voice and her sister Margaret's. She heard the barking of the old dog that was chained to the sycamore tree" (109). In the scene, the sounds and visuals fade. Particularly, the presence of her family is diluted into the sea as the scene draws to a close. Edna's depiction in the last scene, then, can be seen as the representation of liberation. The use of sensations here is also important. The narrator intends to have the reader experience Edna's fading and disappearance. She, then, finally overcomes her last barrier by entering the sea, a patriarchal domain. However, Edna's suicide is, to some extent, incomprehensible, suggesting other alternative perspectives. Nonetheless, she, like Tess, is in a state of mental stagnation at the time of her suicide and does not offer another situation to consider. Edna's familiar relationship, as the omniscient narrator unveils, shows the social pressure that eventually becomes convenient for building a naturalistic structure. This dialogue reconstructs the medical thought mentioned by Toril Moi in an analysis of the book *The Law of Heredity* (1883) by W. K. Brooks:

> For Brooks, social differences between the sexes are caused by their psychological differences. ... Moving on to the intellectual differences between men and women, he claims that men's brains enable them to grasp the unknown: discoveries, science, the highest artistic and

philosophical insights. ... Women's brains can deal with the known, the ordinary, and the everyday, keep track of traditions and social customs. (16)

The analysis by this author lets us see the scientific thought of the late nineteenth century about women. It is not a surprise, then, that the women were subject to carry all sorts of deviancies, wrongdoing, sickness, and so forth. However, in the case of Edna Pontellier, the reader would find the character in an ambiguous situation.

Also, these similarities with Flaubertians in his novel *Madame Bovary* (1856) and Chopin confirm the naturalistic perspective and the crafting of realism in Emma Bovary becomes framed in the Naturalism that leads the reader to see, in a vivid way, Emma's motives and actions (Witherow 91). While Edna entangles herself in self-destructive behavior, unlike Emma, she does not seem to have enough of a motive for her suicide (Witherow 91). Edna Pontellier's death is, in fact, difficult to understand because Edna's suicide cannot be explained. This conclusion, she noted, can be reached after carefully surveying several possible real reasons for suicide in Edna's daily life. Cyrille Arnavon discards Robert Lebrun's situation and discards the divorce because she thinks there is a possibility of "reconciliation." The death of Edna Pontellier could be seen as a technique that was in use widely by Naturalism, as in *Santa*, for example. In other words, there are no explicit narrative reasons for Edna's suicide, but the aesthetic reason is Naturalism.

A different explanation of the unusual finale of the novel can be seen through the biographer Daniel Rankin, who refers to the novel as an "autobiographical" account (Arnavon 186). It is important to notice that Naturalism's structure and the concept of determinism are present in the narrative. Moreover, Edna has a strong presence in front of her husband and in front of society, for example, when Mr. Pontellier complains to Doctor Mandelet and expresses that "her whole attitude—toward me and everybody and everything—has changed" (63). He complains that Edna has refused her social contact. He also feels "like thousands of devils after I've made a fool of myself. She's making it devilishly uncomfortable" (63). Edna makes a reference to Doctor Manelet in the last scene, suggesting social isolation: "Good-by—because I love you.' ... He would never understand. Perhaps Doctor Mandelet would understand" (109).

The medical influence is strong and appears to frame the character negatively, like Doctor Moragas in *La piedra angular*, who brings to the reader the character of the murderer. Moragas not only serves as an authority over the body or the psychology of the murderer's character but also participates with the legal authorities and becomes part of them. In Gamboa's narrative, the figure of the doctor becomes a key part of the state's bureaucracy when the main character is in the last decline. In *Santa,* the medical doctor is the voice of the knowledge of the woman's body; he is the only authority who speaks about the biology of the woman. Overall, in these novels, the doctors, all male, act as authorities who diagnose any anomaly in the female characters.

Another circumstance to blame for Edna's suicide is mental illness, as the information appears in several dialogues. It is important to notice that under the medical view, women were prone to, or inclined toward, hysteria, any kind of sickness, and any kind of mental disorder. The narrative illustrates this condition through Doctor Mandelet when he suggests, "Woman, my dear friend, is a very peculiar and delicate organism" (64). This statement brings to light not only the societal interpretation of Edna, but also the medical view of women in the nineteenth century. In regard to medical views of women at the time, Toril Moi's readings of Brooks find tendencies and constructions of inferiority in women represented in sickness or mental issues. The idea of mental illness reiterates the naturalistic view and presentation of the character of Edna Pontellier. Gamboa's character, Santa, is another candidate to see how the main character presents mental illness, though the narrative uses alcohol as a device to frame this problem. María contrasts with Edna and Santa. She does not have weakness or any other illness. The medical discourse does not have a key role and does not intervene with the main character in the novel. Other literary works from England were culturally far from Mexico but maintained a constant literary dialogue with the United States in which the New Woman was present.

Tess of the D'Urbervilles

The British novel *Tess of the D'Urbervilles* brings to the forefront the main character, Tess, who is, in part, crafted with Naturalism aesthetics. The novel addresses the woman's independence and in its depiction of the character, which deals not only with injustice but also with rough living conditions. In other words, the character lives amid adversarial hardships socially, economically, and physically, but despite harsh circumstances, she is still emotionally independent. Thomas Hardy was well known as a writer supportive of feminist ideas about different issues, particularly in regard to sex and marriage. He, as we see in the novel, raises questions similar to those of the other New Woman writers.[42] The feminist view and the ideas of Hardy's female

---

[42] It is important to highlight that Thomas Hardy, no doubt, uses Naturalism in his novel. Simon Joyce in his book *Modernism and Naturalism in British and Irish Fiction 1880-1930* points out that "… when seeking to trace a Zolian influence upon British fiction, Gosse found little to document, beyond Thomas Hardy – and only thein by identifying *Tess of the D'Urbervilles* somewhat narrowly as a "study of Dorsetshire dairy-farms" (7). In other words,

characters coincide with their sexual independence. Tess does not escape from this trend, but under the Victorian view, she is expected to keep her first sexual partner during the time of the events throughout the novel (Brady 94).

Tess's first sexual interaction is through a violent, abusive rape by Alec D'Urberville, though it is a polysemic representation. The most obvious representation of the sexual attack is the patriarchal dominance over women in Victorian times. This is the novel's point of departure to show how Tess falls toward social marginalization, hardship in working conditions, and finally, her death. Her condition worsens after she confesses to Angel her encounter with Alec. In the scene, Angel wants to confess his faults and have Tess forgive him: "He then told her of that time of his life to which allusion has been made when tossed about by doubts and difficulties in London, ... he plunged into eight-and-forty hours' dissipation with a stranger" (286). To this Tess replies,

> 'Oh Angel —I am almost glad —because now you
> can forgive *me!* ...I have a confession, too—remember, I said so.'...
> ... She bent forward, at which each diamond on her neck gave a sinister wink ...;
> [S]he entered on her story of her acquaintance with Alec d'Urberville and its results, murmuring the words without flinching and with her eyelids drooping down. (286-287, emphasis in original)

The dialogue that occurs later not only unbalances the state of power between the men and women in the marriage settings but also marks the beginning of Tess's decay. There is no doubt that Hardy, in this novel, plays with the naturalistic scheme, though Zola's Naturalism was not welcome in England at the time. Sara Beliveau argues that Hardy's Naturalism does not originate from Zola's model. Furthermore, Hardy's case comes from a different culture and literary tradition that does not converge with French Naturalism (Beliveau 110). Class and cultural differences are also present in Angel's attitudes toward marriage and toward his wife. Tess falls into a number of economic and social problems after the scene of "confession." Also, her psychology shows signs of deterioration:

> "But I don't care," she said. "Oh no —I don't care! I will always be ugly now, because Angel is not here, and I have nobody to take care of me ..."

Hardy "somewhat" uses Naturalism or at least nuances of it. Also, as one can notice in the quotes above, the Zolian literary proposal was not very popular in Great Britain.

—Thus, Tess walks on; a figure that is part of the landscape; a field-woman pure and simple in winter guise; a gray serge cape, a red woolen cravat …

—Inside of this exterior … was the record of a pulsing life which had learned too well … of the cruelty of lust and the fragility of love. (357)

In Tess's state of desolation, as we see, the narrator combines the landscape with winter and gray color as a vision of her desolation. Also, her psychological and emotional interior is shown in parallel with these natural visions of the English countryside. Notice that Hardy worked English rural imagery into other works. In fact, after Tess leaves "more than eight months subsequent to the parting of Clare and Tess, "[w]e discover the latter in changed conditions; instead of a bride… we see her a lonely woman… Mentally, she remained in utter stagnation, a condition which the mechanical occupation rather fostered than checked" (347). The psychology of Tess brings us to the idea of emotional and mental decline. As Linda M. Shires states, Tess is left to "nature's laws," in which random events could happen, the women are determined to fall, and any kind of possibility is encountered daily. Notice that the character of Tess is not diluted in sickness as often as it occurs in the Naturalism structure. On the contrary, she disappears because she defended herself.

The ambiguity of Hardy's Naturalism is also present in the novel. Some aspects of Hardy's Tess do not hide their Naturalism, while at the same time, others keep some resonance with Zola's idea of the "experimental" novel (Neil 172). Nonetheless, by taking a deep look at Tess in her final stages, Hardy's story does not end the character because of sickness or mental decline. Tess dies in the midst of juridical actions that put her in an ambiguous position in relation to Naturalism. The narrator presents the situation while stating, "All waited in the growing light, their faces and hands as if they were glistening green-grey… Soon, the light was strong, and a ray shone upon her unconscious form. … 'What is it, Angel?' she said… 'Have they come for me?'… 'Yes, dearest,' he said" (505). The story, nonetheless, presents two versions of the character: Tess, the victim, and Tess, the criminal.

Although in Tess the New Woman's features are not so clear, there are other characteristics that can be accounted for in the narrative. Perhaps the most important one is the divorce or the separation from Angel, which leads to the view of Tess as a strong and independent woman despite the difficulties. Other aspects of the New Woman are presented in Hardy's works. First, most of Hardy's heroines are presented in some way as sexually independent and active (Watts 154). In *Tess*, nonetheless, the double standard of a sexually pure woman is highlighted as a social critique (Watts 155). Other instances of New Woman traits, particularly in narratives, can be found in the decline of the power of male characters. For example, Angel, in the scene of "confession," appears not only surprised but also confused: "These and other of his words were nothing but the perfunctory babble of the surface while the depths remained paralyzed" (292). This image might also converge with other confused men in the New Woman narrative. Also, it is important to mention Alec's murder, in which Tess overcomes not only physical force but also cleverness. Overall, Hardy's novel shares some aspects of French Naturalism, though it is clear that the schematic model of Zola's *femme fatale* does not exist in the novel of Hardy. Tess's death is not derived from her sexual behavior; it happens because she is a victim of the social differences, as we clearly see throughout the novel.

Ideala

Contrasting with Hardy, *Ideala* by Grand explicitly crafts the title character in the New Woman frame, allowing her to initiate a conversation with male dominance. Nonetheless, the narrative through a male narrator creates a perspective that differs from the naturalistic aesthetics. It brings forth a "new male view" of women to be understood. This perspective does not lean on a specific gender. The novel also constructs settings and other parts in a counterpoint to Naturalism. Ideala is a character who not only suffers in many ways in her dysfunctional marriage but also becomes a victim of sickness. The narrator lets us see the genesis of her divorce when he states, "The trouble was her husband. … He was jealous of her, jealous of her popularity, and jealous for everyone who approached her … and was even obliged to be cold and reserved with some of her best friends" (41). In the early stages of the novel, we witness Ideala's private life with her husband, who states clearly what her problem is. Nonetheless, the story presents the title character as a controversial woman who responds cleverly to the male domain when Claudia talks with the narrator: "Ideala is not a common character herself." … Ideala is a much cleverer woman than I am. She would make me laugh at my own advice in five minutes" (135). It is important to mention that education is important to the New Woman. In Sarah Grand's essay "Should Married Women Follow Professions?" she suggests that a woman should pursue a profession, even though she will have difficulties. She also suggests that the household alone is one profession, but that its duties "are looked upon as mere drudgery" (123). Grand's arguments about professional development suggest that a married woman should have the same chance to become a professional. She portrays the household as an obstacle to married women's attainment of professional status, as an activity that promotes self-neglect, and as a comfortable situation when she states that the woman would prefer to find "a nice man to do the work for her" (125).

In relation to other activities, Grand also brings to light not only independence but also the idea of a woman as the same as a man. She criticizes the Bawling Brotherhood, as she states in "The New Aspect of the Woman Question:" (Heilmann and Forward): "Both the cow-woman and the scum-woman are well within the range of the comprehension of the Bawling Brotherhood, but the New Woman is a little above him" (29). She intends for other women to take the wheel of their lives and move on to serious actions for themselves and by themselves. Sarah Grand is not against marriage. She thinks that a problematic marriage is not fearful for a woman, she argues in the essay "Marriage Questions in Fiction." She also adds in this work that passion alone does not mean love (Grand 85).

Ideala is also a social activist in favor of women in regard to equality in many forms, but particularly in regard to marriage:

> 'Marriages are made in Heaven!' the Bishop ejaculated, feebly...
> 'I think an ideal of marriage should be fixed by law, and lectures given in all the colleges to teach it,' Ideala went on; "and a standard of excellence ought to be set up for people to attain to before they could be allowed to marry. They should be obliged to pass examinations on the subject...."
> (137)

The excerpt puts into view two pillars of society represented in the characters of the bishop and the judge. Ideala also questions society, gender, power, and government. In Foucault's discussions on discipline, there appears the notion of what he calls "the swarming of disciplinary mechanisms," which deals with the incensement of the establishment mechanisms by de-institutionalizing and transforming into a series of inquiries about the individual and his/her social, medical, psychological, and other proclivities (Foucault, *Discipline & Punish* 211). The Church, as in Ideala's statements, is a good example of these mechanisms when she suggests that women should have a more active role in marriage. Sarah Grand points out in her essay "The New Aspect of the Woman Question" that "[b]oth the cow-woman and the scum-woman are well within the range of the comprehension of the Bawling Brotherhood, but the New Woman is a little above him" (29). Grand intends for women to sustain themselves and that they should be proactive in many aspects of their lives to overcome their unproductive state. In her essay "Does Marriage Hinder A Woman's Self-Development?" Grand remarks, among other things, about the overly powerful man in marriage and its consequences. She says, "the man is dragged down enough; but he, by the customs of society, can escape to a large extent from the dead weight of his self-inflicted destiny... To the woman, as always, society, having been ordered by a man, has not been quite so kind" (119). A society entirely managed by men is prone to make the women fail and leave them in stagnation.

Grand's novel lets us see how the main character is transformed but not diluted by sickness or even crime: "She gathers the useless unit of society about her and makes them worthy women" (189). Different from other characters of Radical Naturalism, Ideala becomes not only a successful woman for herself but helps other women to succeed regardless of their social position. Nonetheless, Grand's *Ideala* includes a form of Naturalism's structure. The sickness is present in many forms, and some relate to her marriage. Among others is the mental illness caused by her husband's violence (Heilmann, *New Woman Strategies* 49). She recuperates from such an illness: "to one who had borne the heavy winter with a heavy heart but was able at last to lay down a load of care, the transition must have been like a sudden change from painful sickness to perfect health" (91). The resurgence from any sickness elevates her not only physically but also psychologically and emotionally. Teresa Magnum points out that Ideala's marriage leads her to meet the character of Lorimer, and because of this friendship, they become "social outcasts." Divorce is a topic that Sarah Grand writes about with interest: "It is women who suffer the most from the evil effect of any mistaken change in social arrangements" (85). She also highlights the unfairness and inequality in divorce laws for women. While for men, the divorce meant they "were specially licensed" (Magnum 85), for women, the laws were not equitable. Nonetheless, the novel diverges from the naturalistic perspective and changes the structure of a fallen woman into a successful woman.

This narrative, from the narrator or "new man" narrator, opposes the Radical Naturalism perspectives, diluting the *femme fatale* characters. Nonetheless, the protagonist suffers from her husband's double standards, his betrayal, and her illness. Then, after the sickness, she is a social outcast. Although Ideala loses her health, strength, self-esteem, and so forth, a common trait in naturalistic aesthetics, her health recuperates, and she regains most of her virtues. Grand's novel shows important changes in the protagonist. Among others, in her total recovery, she is working with other women when the narrator states, "She gathers the useless unit of society about her and makes them worthy women" (189). Ideala is working with women who are from the lower social strata, who in Victorian times were women affected by unequal laws and a harsh society. The end depicts a counterpoint statement of Naturalism, which brings forward another possible outcome for a woman in the late nineteenth century. These other outcomes can be seen as another aspect of the New Woman's intention to be socially active.

Conclusion

The works explored here do not converge historically as they present different ways to bring forth Naturalism, Radical Naturalism, and New Woman aesthetics. Radical Naturalism arrived late to Mexico, though it is presented by Federico Gamboa in a well-structured piece, *Santa*, in which the female protagonist is entirely diluted by marginality, chaos, and sickness. The protagonist follows a series of events that entangle with the character's detriment. In this sense, she falls into a romantic feeling that leads toward a sexual life. She is expelled from her house, and she falls into prostitution, sickness, and death. In this way, the determinism in the novel is present, showing Santa's deviant features to the excess. These aspects of the narrative line can be seen as patterns of Radical Naturalism.

Contrasting with Gamboa, Pardo Bazán counterpoints Naturalism, Radical Naturalism in particular, using its own structure in which the cultural aspect becomes important too. In *La piedra angular* and in "Tío Terrones," Pardo Bazán returns to the Naturalism scheme to critique the patriarchal power embedded into a positivistic view of the woman. She also uses linguistic resemblances of the rural town in Spain and uses the space as a sensational element to point out its Spanish singularity. Barragán de Toscano proposes the Mexican identity and Catholicism as an agent of cultural expression integrated with gendered views. In particular, the woman heroine accomplishes what the state cannot. In these novels, the node of juxtaposition is the concept of the New Woman, which presents María, La hija del bandido, Tess, Ideala, Petronila, and the convicted woman of *La piedra angular* as women who are not constructed in accordance with the *femme fatale* trope. These characters do not dissolve into social, health, or psychological symptoms, while some of them are successful in many ways.

Under the same node of convergence, in *The Awakening*, Chopin brings along with her Anglo-American background a series of Flaubertian intertextualities in her literary production. Some aspects of Naturalism are present in Chopin's work, as Edna can be seen as the American Emma Bovary. Although, in the novel, Edna dies, she sets herself free from her marriage, and her husband's power no longer affects her in any way. The character, nonetheless, is progressive. Chopin's work also deviates from the Naturalism aesthetics and supports a feminist perspective. Similarly, in Thomas Hardy's *Tess of the D'Urbervilles*, the novel swings between Naturalism and the New Woman perspective. The main character, Tess, is a paradoxical element that not only shows that determinism is not intrinsically connected to women but also demonstrates that women do not need a man to be able to survive. Another author who relates to the New Woman node is Sarah Grand with her novel *Ideala*. The novel presents harsh critiques of social, state, and religious institutions. Grand develops the character of Ideala, who lives in an environment in which society has a harsh social gaze that affects her in many ways. Nonetheless, she survives and cures herself physically, emotionally, and psychologically despite many adversities. The narrative also frames the theme of marriage not only as a negative and controversial element but also as a cultural one. Part of Grand's argument regarding marriage is related to the unfairness that women receive, particularly the divorce laws, which give extensive advantages to men. These works depict the Spanish, Latin American, and English society's interactions with women at the *fin de siècle*.

The Transatlantic perspective brings together the two sides of the Atlantic to a conversational mode in which the New Woman and Naturalism were present at the time. Giles, Slettedahl, Susan Manning, and Andrew Taylor analyze the connection in some of the works above in the search for homogeneities, observations, connections, and promotion of comparisons among the texts from each side of the Atlantic. Giles points out the conversation among the texts from Transatlantic countries in contextual, historical, and cultural nodes. The philosophical framing of Foucault, Mayer, Moi, Tsuchiya, Showalter, and Dijkstra in the novels of authors from Mexico, Spain, the United States, and England unveils the mechanisms of control of patriarchal power. In all these countries, devices exist that are active in the texts referenced here. The mechanisms, in particular, came mostly from a positivist ideology that helped construct the idea of women as deviant beings, which was used to create the *femme fatale* trope, a scheme. This trope was also used as an anti-establishment literary device by Refugio Barragán de Toscano, Emilia Pardo Bazán, Kate Chopin, Sarah Grand, and Thomas Hardy. This trope, nonetheless, needs a space to inhabit, which is another important aspect used by Naturalism to develop the fate of its characters. In the following chapter, this work will address the topic of space and the place in the novels of Hardy, Gamboa, Barragân de Toacano, Chopin, and Pardo Bazán.

Chapter 2

Women throughout Alternative Spaces and Liminality in Mexican, Spanish, American and British Literatures

Many of the late-nineteenth-century literary works tend to feature negative representations of women. The nature of these depictions varies, but they originated from the idea of women as biologically inferior to men. For example, "…medicine tended to pathologize and criminalize female sexuality" (Heilmann, *New Woman Fiction* 90). These visions converge with the representations of women in literary works from the United States, Great Britain, Spain, and Mexico. Literature at the *fin de siècle* adopted different perspectives. Radical Naturalism derives from Naturalism, which was mostly used in Latin America and in Spain. Alternatively, the New Woman perspective criticized the social construction of women and the role of marriage as their only goal to accomplish in their lives. Writers with this point of view used the fate of marginal characters to mark them as agents of change. The two points of view established a conversation based on gender and were reflected in female characters and in the social space they occupied. Many places with different boundaries in the novels below became relevant for representations of women because of the power relations among the characters. Thus, these spaces are part of the *vis-a-vis* between Radical Naturalism and the New Woman. In addition, reviewing different spaces will reveal how the settings construct a liminal place in which gender relations and patriarchal power reverse.

This chapter explores how spaces of the brothel, the cave, the countryside, the inn, and the house connect female characters with crime and liminality in the novels of *Santa* (1903) by Federico Gamboa from Mexico; *La hija del bandido o los subterráneos del nevado* (1887), by Refugio Barragán de Toscano from Mexico; *La gota de sangre* (1911), by Emilia Pardo Bazán from Spain; *Tess of the D'Urbervilles: A Pure Woman* (1891), by Thomas Hardy from Great Britain; and *The Awakening* (1899), by Kate Chopin from the United States.

Definitions

To avoid confusion and to maintain a coherent analysis, the following terms and concepts used in this chapter need to be explained. Crime can be defined as any act that goes against civil and/or criminal laws. Deviancy refers to a specific sexual behavior that goes beyond the social norm(s). The concept comes from a code made by the state or by society that regulates sexuality and marriage for men and women. Deviancies include a lack of adherence to social roles, often considered criminal. Representational space is an object that is expressed in different ways, and in order to be evoked, it must exist somewhere. This concept is abstract, and it appears in literary works when they represent the space with its own particular nuances and measurements.[1] (Ingardern 222). The notion of a place (for example, the patio, the house, the countryside, the country, or a continent) is less abstract because it can be named. All these places can be considered part of the representational space defined above, which resonates in literary works. The discussion in this chapter needs the philosophical background of the topics mentioned above. The next section will explain the theoretical framework of the spaces, such as the brothel, the cave, the countryside, the inn, and the house.

Framework

Paul Giles brings to light the discrepancies of the idea of homogeneity in literature from the United States and Great Britain that was/is not only frequent but also active in many cultural aspects. Robert Weisbuch defines "cultural time" as "the collective metaphor that expresses an age's view of itself in relation to all of history. It is not only a reflection of a historical attitude; once established, it directs and helps to determine perceptions beyond a strictly historical field" (97). Therefore, a historical approach by itself does not suffice to frame the culture of America or England. All these points can also adequately frame differences (e.g., historical or stylistic) in the literary works from Spain and Mexico. Weisbuch suggests, at the *fin de siècle*, that cultural idiosyncrasies reveal the lack of homogeneity in literary works across the Atlantic's physical space, which is also an ideological place.

---

[1] Roman Ingardern, in his book *The Literary Work of Art* states: "If in a literary work there are represented objects that are 'real' according to their content, and if their reality type is to be preserved, they must be represented as existing in time and space or even as being spatial in themselves. ... Thus, when the author of a novel 'transports' us from place *A* to place *B* without showing us the entire distance between *A* and *B*, the intervening space between *A* and *B* is not positively determined and represented but ... is only corepresented, by virtue of the impossibility of spatial discontinuity. Explicitly, truly represented space is as if pocked with gaps, which show up as, so to speak, spots of indeterminacy.... Here we come upon a characteristic trait of represented objects in general ..." (222-224; emphasis in original).

Similarities in the way we see the space can be found in different theorists. For example, Edward Said highlights how cultural identities relate themselves through a constructed or "man-made" idea of a spatial division between orient and occident rather than through other connections with historical perceptions. The sense of ideological and physical space appears in Northrop Frye's notion of the archetype. He explains how the archetype (e.g., the figure of the hero) is a cultural iteration that is constantly present in literary works throughout time and place (Frye 137). It is important to notice that the cultural aspect of these novels can also be related with Frye's idea of cultural archetypes. In a tangential position, Michel Foucault explains that some social spaces can be designed for deviance, ritual, or odd behaviors that are non-normative. Society, then, would not only see or interact with these behaviors but also control them. He also suggests that these behaviors were, and are, controlled through the observation in which the panopticon is essential.

In reference to women, Bram Dijkstra shows how fantasies about women at the end of the nineteenth century reflected the male disposition throughout visual arts with negative tropes (e.g., "collapsed women," "sleeping women," or "sirens"). These representations are always connected with the space these women occupy in paintings, literature, and so forth. Similarly, Toril Moi points out that during the nineteenth century, the positivist perspective undermined women throughout philosophy and the biological sciences. Women were depicted with fewer physical and/or psychological capabilities. A woman, however, Moi points out, is a subjective definition. In addition, Orlando Patterson lets us see how the rite of social death and its intrinsic connection with liminality works not only in the social and geographical space but also at a human level. Following the idea of liminality, Van Arnol Gennep explains how liminal states and spaces are embedded with rites in religious, political, social, or spiritual contexts. These theoretical frames will help one to understand the space, the female characters, crime, and liminality in the aforementioned novels. In the next section, I lay out relevant literature for this chapter.

Criticism

Fin de siècle Mexican literature is the focus of numerous scholars with different points of view who study novels from diverse theoretical perspectives. Here is a survey of the principal scholars who examine the space in Mexican novels such as *Santa* and *La hija del bandido*. Jennifer Shade Venegas successfully addresses a series of spaces and emphasizes the brothel as a heterotopic space. She indicates that the brothel, in particular, brings to the fore the idea of a marginalized place in which deviant women are welcome. She adds how liminality is present in the character of Santa and how it becomes visual because she has access to marginal and non-marginal places. Ana María

Alvarado points out that the brothel is a prominent space in the novel that evokes national decadence and corruption. Although both articles identify the relation between the space and other elements of the novel, they fail to make other connections. The first does not address Santa's house as another heterotopic space or the ritual aspect of liminality. The second, by Alvarado, does not mention aspects of liminality. Debra A. Castillo writes about how the narrators become a concomitant part of the author. She unveils how the story uses Santa as a rhetorical construction of the fallen woman and points out how Radical Naturalism as a male aesthetic product can be interpreted from the feminist perspective as a "re-genderification of the text" (Castillo 176).

Rodrigo Cánovas studies the main character and the Radical Naturalism discourse in his essay. He illuminates these aspects of Gamboa's novel extensively. He addresses the aspect of Naturalism of the novel and how the main character is degraded in different ways. Additionally, he discusses the main character as an allegory of the nation, but he does not extend his study further to social death or a liminal perspective. Alternatively, Javier Ordiz studies the countryside of *Santa* and its symbolic connections with nation-building and political contexts. He also emphasizes the role of the main character as a symbol of the nation. Additionally, the urban space in Mexico City between 1890 and 1930 was a battleground for dominance among the municipality, peddlers, and beggars, as Pablo Piccato unveils. He examines how prostitution and other deviances were treated. Katherine E. Bliss argues that legal battles to regulate prostitution led to its criminalization after 1918. She mentions other marginal subjects. María Zalduono locates the link between women and banditry from different perspectives. She expertly identifies themes of nation-building, gender, and banditry in the structure of the novel by drawing connections to broader Latin American literature of the time. For example, she suggests that the type of narrative allows the novel to connect with different spaces throughout. She also looks into the banditry in nineteenth-century Mexican literature. Similarly, Nancy LaGreca addresses the characters of Vicente Colombo and María from the Lacanian view and from Kristeva's psychoanalytic perspective. Furthermore, she extends her argument into space, crime and liminality.

The Spanish novel *La gota de sangre* sparks curiosity about crime, the fallen woman, and Madrid in various studies. Fernando J. Barroso studies Pardo Bazán's uses of Naturalism. He explores the arrival of Naturalism to Spain and how Pardo Bazán not only presents it but also implements it in her literary production. According to Barroso, her works in the late nineteenth and early twentieth century offered plenty of naturalistic scenarios. In her criticism, she explains how Naturalism fails to prove the causes of human acts. Fernando Vicente Albarrán tackles the space from a historical perspective. He studies how the path of modernization exposes tensions, resistance, anxieties, and marginalities. Albarrán brings to the fore the *Ensanche*, which was the way to name the act of modernization of Madrid. The *Ensanche* was key for social development in Madrid at the time. Nonetheless, modernization is easily perceived in Pardo Bazán's novels and short stories. Jesus Filgueira Ganzo suggests that Pardo Bazán uses polarities to make references to realities outside the text or as a form of symbolism. He highlights the binary terms civilization and barbarism used by Pardo Bazán to reference Madrid as the center of knowledge in Spain. Hence, Jean-Luis Guereña provides a good view of the legal landscape during the late nineteenth century concerning prostitution in Spain. While this variety of essays helps contextualize crime, women, or history, it misses references to liminality, though it is important to mention that some sources come from the field of history.

Spaces, gender, deviancies, and the liminal subject are essential elements in Chopin's novel *The Awakening* discussed by Elmo Howell, Wenhui Hong, Molly Hildebrand, and Armantine M. Smith. Elmo Howell studies creole women and their legal situation in Louisiana, as they were subject to many constraints. He finds how these constrains are related to Chopin's novel. Armantine M. Smith examines how women were tied to their spouses and how husbands could abuse them psychologically and socially whenever the wives would overstep their constraints. Smith suggests that in labor settings, women in Louisiana were not allowed to work as independent individuals. Wenhui Hong claims that gender and space are related in Chopin's novel. Regarding the space in the novel, he states that it is a central element with different representations. For example, he suggests that Grande Isle is a natural and social barrier to continental space that can be understood as a "female utopia." Other spaces and places are mostly patriarchal domains, particularly the house. Molly Hildebrand agrees with Hong because she considers the sea to be an allegory of white male dominance in the art field in which Edna participates. Furthermore, she addresses the suicide of Edna at sea alone as gaining her right to live and die alone. Both studies pay a great deal of attention to the relation between the space and the women, while they do not mention liminality.

Tess of the D'Urbervilles makes connections among certain spaces, liminality, and female characters. The novel has been studied extensively from different theoretical perspectives. William Siebenschuh explains that some spaces and places in the Wessex world of Thomas Hardy are connected to the historical background of England. Similarly, Bertrand C. A. Windle suggests that because of the historical connection to the spaces described in Hardy's works, the reader would be interested in visiting these places. This interest caused a pilgrimage to South England. Windle also examines how the novel gives specific information about where the events occur. Judith R. Walkowitz analyses the urban space (London in particular) during the Victorian era and how the city was a target among writers interested in marginal subjects. Alongside other topics, Walkowitz reveals differences in the legal and moral regulation of prostitution and the interaction among prostitutes, the police, and society.

At the same time, Thomas Hardy argues that his intention with the characters is to depict a sketch of humanity in Wessex and illustrate the customs of the characters. Simon Gatrell highlights the Middle Ages background of the West Saxon. John Sutherland explores the legal aspect of the sexual assault of Alec d'Urbervilles toward Tess and claims that in the historical context, there is "consent" by Tess. Melanie Williams disagrees with Sutherland while looking at the law and points out that there is a case for rape. Nicola Lacey suggests that since Tess let Alec flirt with her and has been flattered by him, she has put herself in danger in the Victorian context. Lacey suggests that the narrative constructs the space in the context of crime, which allows the events to happen. Rosanna Nunan writes about the Victorian view of purity and how it affected the environment. So, spaces such as the city were considered to be in a degenerative process, while rural space was viewed as racially pure. Nunan also studies in depth the relation between Victorian philosophical positivism and the perspective of the character of Angel. The combination of all these studies provides a useful context for the space, crime, and women not only in Hardy's novel but also in the context of the house.

The House, the Inn, the Cave, the Brothel, and the Countryside

The Inn in *Tess*

In *Tess of the D'Urbervilles* the house is not a prominent space for criminal occurrences. Outside Tess's house and in other spaces such as the inns or cottages, crime and social deviancies such as alcoholism tend to occur. Early in the novel, the protagonist crosses different parts of Wessex in a pilgrimage-like action. In this space, there are three places that are common for the characters to gather: the cottages, the inns, and the countryside. Wessex is a vast region in which the text intends to depict human nature (Hardy, "General Preface to the Novels and Poems" viii). This place has characters continually moving around while each character travels and stays in places as temporary housing. The countryside is not only the most crucial space in which principal events happen but also a reference to real places in Great Britain. Boundaries of the countryside are difficult to establish in the novel, but it is clear in the novel that the land does not belong to the lower classes. Nonetheless, this space has different concurrences and gatherings of people from different social strata. On the other hand, the cottages/inns are places where the people either live, stay temporarily while working on different activities, or just drink ale. One example is the Rolliver's Inn:

> Rolliver's Inn, the single alehouse at this end of the long and broken village, could only boast of an off-license ... the amount of overt accommodation for consumers was strictly limited to a little board about six inches wide.... In a large bedroom upstairs, the window of which was thickly curtained ..., were gathered ... nearly a dozen persons all seeking beatitude. (26)

The design of this cottage/inn clearly shows the lower social class. This type of scenery is common across the Wessex space, not only in the novel but also in Hardy's other stories.

Contrasting with Rolliver's inn, the narrative emphatically depicts The Herons Inn as a rich aristocratic place frequented by a high-end social class. It is here, in this space, where the crime event occurs. The text not only lets the reader see another aspect of the main character but also takes distance from the fate that Naturalism offers.[2] The story uses the space and a witness narrative to present Tess's crime and, at the same time, explains how it juxtaposes Alec D'Urbervilles' sexual attack. The reader knows that The Herons is mostly used by aristocratic or rich people when Angel speaks with the postal worker, "'That's it!' cried Clare.... 'What place is The Herons? / 'A stylish lodging-house.'... The Herons, though an ordinary villa, stood in its own grounds, and was certainly the last place in which one would have expected to find lodgings, so private was its appearance" (482). The story emphasizes the view of this space as one in which odd behavior or marginal behavior may occur. Heterotopias are spaces that have been designated for deviancies, rituals, sickness, sexual behavior, other odd behaviors, and so forth. Here, the rich and aristocratic people confront a criminal woman they created. The place helps the reader to understand how Victorian values are embedded in the character of Tess and how they were eroded by Alec. In both inns, the women are not restricted by the social constructions, while in the Rolliver's, women drink alcohol freely. In The Herons, a crime had happened.

---

[2] Simon Joyce in his book *Modernism and Naturalism in British and Irish Fiction, 1880-1930* explains the difficulties of locating Naturalism in Victorian fiction. He suggests that what was called realism at the end of nineteenth century in British fiction was embedded with the notion of "documentary effect" which at the time "really means naturalism here" (13). Furthermore, he points out that "realism" has a "habitual deployment as practically a synonym for the Victorian novel *tout court*: in this sense, ... there is no pure realism to be found in ...Hardy ..." (13).

48

Alternatively, the narrator injects the perspective of Mrs. Brooks into The Herons to present Alec's killing and to highlight the physical sensations of the crime and Tess:

> Then the door of the room above was shut, and Mrs. Brooks knew that Tess had re-entered her apartment....
> She accordingly ascended the stairs softly, and stood at the door of the front room—a drawing-room connected with the room immediately behind it ... This first floor, containing Mrs. Brooks's best apartments, had been taken by the week by the d'Urbervilles. The back room was now in silence; but from the drawing-room there came sounds.
> All that she could at first distinguish of them was one syllable, continually repeated in a low note of moaning, as if it came from a soul bound to some Ixionian wheel
> 'O–O–O!' /
> Then a silence, then a heavy sigh, and again –
> 'O–O–O!' / The landlady looked through the keyhole. (485-486)

Tess's actions in this space are uncommon for a woman in the context of the nineteenth century under the Victorian view. Here, by presenting Tess's crime in The Herons through the senses of Mrs. Brooks, the story shows two critical aspects of the characters. First, the character of Mrs. Brooks contextualizes the situation of the event. Thus, the reader is aware of the space and the events through her hearing, her views, and her thoughts. Moreover, in this scene, the role of Tess changes from that of a victim to that of a heroin. At the same time, the main character disrupts the idea of the fallen woman. Tess's crime, then, becomes a liberator and ambiguous element.

Second, Mrs. Brooks's interest in the d'Urbervilles' room relates to the concept of "the control of activity" that Foucault suggests. This concept involves observations of the other and policing them while regularizing patterns of behavior. Whenever these patterns change, they are subject to be investigated, punished, or reprimanded. This control also includes religious scrutiny along with moral views. In this novel, these observations operate at the inn, an enclosed space that illustrates the Foucauldian concept of "control of activity." The crime, on the other hand, is one of the passions that occurs inside the inn's room to which the reader has no access (Lacey 5). It represents the peak of tension in the novel. This climax elicits a catharsis of justice and predisposes empathy in the reader toward Tess. Although, according to the law, Tess is a criminal, the narrative gives the reader a different perspective, highlighting a sense of justice. Through this space, the story creates an alternative path for Tess, and it changes her fate as a character, a narrative element that is characteristic of the New Woman's point of view. The novel engages the reader in a deep social and legal discourse in which the balance of justice in Tess prevails.

The Herons' geography facilitates a heterotopic space that allows different transgressions to occur by Tess or Alec. In this heroic moment, the narrative includes the idea of trickery, as Tess talks to herself to avoid Mrs Brooks getting into the room. Trickery refers to an ingenious hero, like Odysseus, in the cave. In this sense, the novel agrees with the archetypes of the literature of Northrop Frye. It evokes, at least, the Greek hero, not to mention other heroes that come after. As in many of these narratives, the space, mostly the enclosed space, is a relevant element that helps the hero(ine) to perform all his abilities.

The Countryside in *Tess*

Hardy's *Tess* uses the resources of the countryside not only to add symbolism, make historical connections, or frame crime but also to enhance the situations endured by the main character. Here in this novel, the countryside is also a patriarchal domain in which the characters of women are exploited and abused. The best example is the sexual abuse of Tess by Alec d'Urbervilles. Although there are many discrepancies in interpretations of Alec's sexual advances toward Tess in The Chase, the scene, no doubt, explains the role of rural women in Great Britain. The visions of the rape, as a crime or not, are notably common interpretations of the event, but the text lets one see that Tess does not totally agree with Alec, "'How could you be so treacherous!' said Tess, between archness and real dismay, and getting rid of his arm by pulling open his fingers one by one, though at the risk of slipping off herself" (87). The narrator presents the scene to the readers, allowing them to infer that Tess prefers to fall rather than to let Alec help her. Moreover, following this line of actions, the story adds an ambience of sensations when Alec attacks Tess:

> Darkness and silence ruled everywhere around. Above them rose the primeval yews and oaks of The Chase, in which were poised gentle roosting birds.... But might some say where was Tess's guardian angel? where was the providence of her simple faith? Perhaps, like that other god of whom the ironical Tishbite spoke, he was talking, or he was pursuing, or he was in a journey (90-91)

These invocations of the "guardian angels" by themselves outline Tess's vulnerability in front of Alec. In a deviation from Radical Naturalism, Tess is depicted as a victim. The space of the countryside favors male dominance, and the narrative gives a characterization of the landscape to demonstrate such power. The sensation of darkness suggests a negative aspect of the countryside that facilitates Alec's advances. Moreover, in the scenes of The Chase, Hardy uses, directly or indirectly, two tropes of the visual culture of Victorian times. The first is the "collapsing woman" or the "sleeping woman," who not only represents the woman's exhaustion from masturbation and the male voyeuristic erotic attraction (Dijkstra 70). The novel visually alerts the reader to Alec's desires while Tess is sleeping alone in The Chase, "'Tess!' said d'Urberville. / There was no answer … Everything else was blackness…. He knelt and bent lower, till her breath warmed his face. … She was sleeping soundly …" (90). The sleeping woman represents an individual as a decorative element that, in the case of the Victorian point of view, was the functional state of a woman as a mother and as support for the husband. The second is the woman as a virginal entity, as nature is depicted many times covered in leaves and/or with various children surrounding the woman's body; it is a representation of nature "as the all-giving, all-receiving womb" (Dijkstra 85). The character of Alec prepares the settings that result in a nature-like representation: "She passively sat down amid the leaves he had heaped and shivered….With the setting of the moon, the pale light lessened, and Tess became invisible …" (89). Alec and his desires are the representation of patriarchy, making invisible the body of the woman, particularly when sexuality is involved. This invisibility dehumanizes women. In this open space in the countryside, Tess becomes part of the nature males dominate, allowing Alec to abuse her. Alternatively, this depiction of Tess can be compared with the concept of the woman as an "all-giving and all-receiving" entity. Alec becomes the prototype of the Victorian rich or aristocratic male.

Contrary to Hardy's depictions, in England at the end of the century, the rural zones were considered by "purity activists" to be morally pure. Their inhabitants and dwellers were compared with the urban population when the city became an immoral place where sexual life was out of control. In the city, venereal disease was very common and plagued the urban social landscape, affecting the entire range of the social structure (Nunan 294). Tess, as the novel's title suggests, is "a pure woman," referring to the purity in health and morality corrupted by male domination in rural England. It is the same patriarchal dominance that appears in the countryside of *La hija*, in which the bandit's grounds are the rural landscape. In this novel, for example, the kidnapping of Cecilia occurs late at night in the rural town. In the novel, the band of Vicente Colombo dominates in all senses. He, as in *El Zarco* of Altamirano, is a bandit who is recognized as a civil and political authority in the rural landscape and all the towns that surround it. He replaces the authority of the state. Women in the novel also have no prominence in criminal activity. Within this landscape, María is the exception.

As in Hardy's novel, the countryside plays an essential role as a space for patriarchal dominance. In the Mexican narrative across the Atlantic, in *La hija* and *Santa*, depictions of male dominance in the countryside abound. They frame the female characters mostly as victims of patriarchy's norms and behaviors, as we see with the Pedregal in *Santa*. In *Tess*, the name of the wood, The Chase, and the darkness that covers the scene help Alec's sexually predatory intentions. They also bring to the front the arbitrary and uneven power structures among the aristocracy, the educated middle class, and the lower class. In *La hija*, the countryside is the battleground between good and evil, leaving the former for the male overpowering the landscape in the novel. By allowing strange sexual behaviors and other odd behaviors, these spaces converge with Foucault's concept of heterotopias mentioned above. They also participate in other spaces as part of political, economic, social, and cultural conversations. For example, the countryside in Hardy's novel allows the reader to see how social classes and male dominance over women worked as cultural or social practices. And so, the novels' representations bring to the conversation the Victorian rich and aristocratic man. As mentioned above, in *Tess*, the countryside plays a vital role in depicting different social and biological anomalies. Characters move along sites, towns, inns, or cottages in the vast Wessex landscape as they are exposed to a series of daily life experiences (Hardy, "General Preface to the Novels and Poems" viii). The narrative follows these situations as it raises gender, social, political, and/or philosophical questions throughout the story. Deviancies, in this context, draw a contrast between Victorians' vision of sexuality and the daily rural lived experience. A particular scene presents a gathering through Tess's perspective by guiding the reader through interminable music and dancing in which maids from Trantridge interact socially with aristocratic young men, such as Alec d'Urbervilles. Alec explains to Tess how this gathering works:

> 'The maids don't think it respectable to dance at "The Flower-de-Luce,"'
> 'he explained. 'They don't like to let everybody see which be their fancy-men.' Besides the house sometimes shuts up just when their jints begins to get greased. So, we come here and send out for liquor.' (78)

Alec's explanation unveils the constant relationship between aristocratic men and countryside girl workers. These types of gatherings are customary in Trantridge. The excerpt reveals two aspects of Tess. First, other characters recognize Tess's detachment from the events, "Don't ye be nervous, my dear good soul, expostulated, between his coughs, a young man with a wet face....What's yerr hurry? To-morrow is Sunday thank God, and we can sleep it off in church time" (78). These characters' perceptions include Alec when he approaches her and asks, "Well, my Beauty, what are you doing here?" (79). Second, Tess does not fit here because she does not feel at home. She is foreign in all this space: "She became restless and uneasy; yet, having waited so long, it was necessary to wait longer.... She did not abhor dancing, but she was not going to dance here" (78).

In other words, Tess does not belong to this space, in which disparate social and sexual behaviors are obviously present. This lack of belonging is true not only from her perspective but also from that of other characters. This estrangement underlines the relationship between Tess, "a pure woman," as the epitome of Victorian virtues and her perception of other characters. In particular, other female characters differ from Tess because they do understand the situation and feel comfortable interacting with aristocratic males.

Alternating these perspectives, the narrator includes natural elements to stress the oddity of the space:

> It was a windowless erection used for storage, and from the open door there floated into the obscurity a mist of yellow radiance, which at first Tess thought to be illuminated smoke. But ... it was a cloud of dust, lit by candles within the outhouse ...
> When she came close and looked in she beheld indistinct forms racing up and down to the figure of the dance, the silence of their footfalls arising from their being overshoe in 'scroff'– that is to say, the powdery residuum from the storage of peat and other products, the stirring of which by their turbulent feet created the nebulosity that involved the scene. (77)

The sequence of the events is placed in an obscure, nebulous environment to allow peculiar relations in this section. It shows a dissimilar relationship between aristocratic men and rural girls, "They don't like to let everybody see which be their fancy-men" (78). These gatherings alone, in the Victorian view, could be considered abnormal behavior. In addition, this part suggests sexual encounters between them: "[T]he fresh night air was producing staggering and serpentine courses among the men who had partaken too freely; some of the more careless women also were wandering in their gait" (80). The creation of this space, then, involves social class, gender, sexuality, and political questions (Lefebvre 70) that resonated at the *fin de siècle* in Great Britain. It represents the place relegated by society for odd sexual and/or odd social behaviors. This is a prostitution-like spectacle that contrasts with social and political tensions raised by controlling prostitution in Great Britain at the time (Walkowitz 23). The countryside recreates an appropriated space changed into a heterotopia as a space of leisure and a brothel-like place.

The Cave in *La hija*

A variation of the house as a form of a cave appears in the Mexican novel *La hija del bandido*. As in other novels, the cave takes the functions of the house. It is a protective, enclosed place. We see this function when Vicente Colombo,

María's father, states, "The poor girl [María] lives constantly kept, not by thick bars of iron, but by an impenetrable rock, where only the eagle nests, and where all the police investigations will always crash" (7).[3] Colombo's explanation not only makes clear the relation between María and the cave as a house and fortress but also condenses the tensions of the novel. María lives in this place in a state of innocence, but she is surrounded by the cruelest banditry. At the same time, the cave is a dark and dangerous place, as it is described by the narrator when Colombo visits a kidnapped person in the cave:

> ...[A]nd almost crawling ... [,] he crossed a subterranean room to its end ... [It]had the shape of a perfect square. That cave ... was worthy of study, because of its well-polished walls.... At the center of one of the walls, coming out of the rock, [was] a sort of a nose about nine inches thick a hole drilled through each side and a rope crossed horizontally from side to side with the ends tied together[.] All was formed toward the center of the cave in which a thick hawser was disappearing into a hole ... Our man descended very quickly like a Ferris wheel bucket (8-9)[4]

In essence, part of the space is a hole in a cave, and the hole leads to a sort of confined place in which Colombo, his daughter, and his band live. It is a place where Colombo's unconscious shows up. In this space, the *id* appears to let us see how deep-rooted in evilness are Colombo's thoughts, sentiments, instincts, and desires. It is the "third" level of the human psyche. It represents the inner and repressed desires, thoughts, feelings, or urges (Siegfried 2). The way in which this place is well polished and constructed not only reveals Colombo's dark inner thoughts or instincts but also shows how well-crafted are his plans to abandon banditry and become a notable person in society. The cave, nonetheless, is an ambiguous place in which evil and good coexist. It is a grave and yet protects María, as her mother writes:

---

[3] "La pobre niña vive siempre guardada, si no por espesas rejas de hierro, si por rocas impenetrables, donde sólo el águila anida, y donde habrán de estrellarse siempre todas las pesquisas de la policía" (7).

[4] "...y casi arrastrándose ... atravesó un subterráneo, a cuyo término ... tenía la figura de un cuadrado perfecto. Aquella cueva ... era digna de estudio, por lo bien pulido de sus paredes ... En el centro de una de éstas, sobresalía, de la misma roca, una especie de nariz como de una[s] nueve pulgadas de espesor y atravesada de lado a lado horizontalmente por un taladro por cada uno de estos taladros, pasaba una soga, cuyos extremos, unidos uno y otros, formaban hacia el centro de la cueva, un grueso calabrote, que iba perderse en un agujero abierto en el centro de aquella ... nuestro hombre descendió tan rápidamente como un cubo de noria" (8-9).

I do not want to go unnoticed all the beauties that were presented in front of my eyes, and the ones that I still remember from this black grave in which I find myself. In all my surroundings, a smiling nature was emerging, with its great green robes, splashed with purple lady birds, yellows, and whites; five-leaf stars, wild zampazúchiles, blue teasels, a hundred colors, lilies. (21)[5]

The purpose of the cave extends from the house or the grave to its primary objective, to hide. The cave is dominated by Vicente in its totality. In this space, Vicente Colombo keeps himself, his daughter, and his loot out of the authorities' view. In other words, the cave protects, hides, and allows crime and death. The place is a fortress, and its impenetrability is intrinsically connected with Colombo's omniscient authority and represents his patriarchal power. The cave gives different alternatives to the narrative that take advantage of its polysemic possibilities.

As an enclosed space that offers security to María, it becomes the perfect place to end her father's authority. This event happens in the famous scene when she drugs the bandits inside the cave during "the first interview that she had with her father, after coming back to that subterranean dwelling ..." (139).[6] She tricks her father first. Then, by her orders, Martín, one of the bandits loyal to María, gives the opium to the band: "María took a closer look at each of those men; finishing her examination, she said in a soft voice – The opium has taken its effect, Martín" (141).[7] It is important to highlight that María creates the plan to tear down her father as a bandit. She acts as a bandit to redeem herself and erase the banditry in the town and its surroundings while changing the male authority toward the female. The cave puts the character of María in a prominent position while emphasizing her bravery and common sense. She becomes a heroine. This female character is an archetype of trickery, a structure found in myths and in other literary products such as romance, tragedy, and so on. This structure is also common in Realism and even in Romanticism. For example, it is present in the works of Conrad, Poe, Virginia Woolf, and other authors (Frye 139-140). The cave in this novel, then, is another element that

---

[5] "No quiero pasar desapercibidas las bellezas que se presentaron entonces a mis ojos, y las que recuerdo desde la negra tumba en que me encuentro. En torno mío se levantaba una naturaleza sonriente, con su magnífico ropaje verde, salpicado de catarinas moradas, amarillas, y blancas; estrellas de cinco hojas, zampazúchiles silvestres, escobetillas azules, cien colores, lirios" (21).

[6] "... la primera entrevista que tuvo con su padre, al tornar de nuevo a aquella morada subterránea ..." (139).

[7] "María estudió separadamente a cada uno de aquellos hombres; y terminando su examen, dijo a media voz: "– El opio ha hecho su efecto; guía, Martín!" (141).

participates in other epic narratives, an archetypal structure of the underworld with patterns found in works such as *The Aeneid, Divine Comedy*, and *Orpheus*, among others.

The House in *The Awakening*

Alternatively to *La hija*, to *Tess*, or to *Santa*, *The Awakening* constructs a house in which the negative perspective toward a woman grows slowly. The narrative line accurately presents the house as a place with a heavy patriarchal presence. Although normativity seems to be present in the house, on a specific night, the house becomes weak in male authority, and dominance loosens as Edna awakens:

> It was Saturday night. ... An unusual number of husbands, fathers, and friends had come down to stay over Sunday; and they were being suitable entertained. ... The dining tables had all been removed to one end of the hall, and the chairs ranged about in rows ... Each little family group had its say about and exchanged its domestic gossip. ... There was now an apparent disposition to relax ... Many of the children had been permitted to sit up beyond their usual bedtime. The little Pontellier boys were permitting them to do so, and making their authority felt. (23)

In this excerpt, the house changes its main role as the place for the family. It transforms into an informal place in which the masculine authority is lost. In this place, the patriarchal representation of authority, "husbands, fathers, and friends" (23), loses its value. This depiction shows a male stereotype that does not belong to the time. Hong suggests that the house falls under male dominance and constraints, a commentary that gains relevance in this discussion. His comments on the house show how Edna challenges the male authority in this domain while she detaches from it and how this leads her to be seen as a deviant. Moreover, the pre-and post-awakening of Edna Pontellier shows what Toril Moi suggests is the answer to the question, "What is a woman?" The answer to this question is a subjective event in which each person answers differently. In this case, we find a firm Edna in search of liberation and disagreeing with patriarchal dominance. As in *La hija*, the authority is turned upside down, empowering the female character to follow her own path, even if she looks like a deviant. The house is the link between Edna and her awakening. Although Edna's house no doubt helps to put the woman in a prominent position, it also allows Edna to deviate from social norms. This motif also appears in other New Woman literary works. In addition, the heterotopic atmosphere in Edna's house is evident, while male authority fails.

The House in *La gota de sangre*

La gota de sangre not only explores naturalistic aesthetics but also converges with the structure of the detective genre through its representation of society, women, and crime in certain spaces. In the storyline, the house plays a vital role regarding crime, women, and aristocracy. The main character of the novel is a misogynistic male who becomes involved in a criminal investigation of a female character, Chulita Ferna (Julia Fernandina). At some point, the reader learns that she is a fallen woman, and the narrator presents her house and its neighborhood as significant places. Julia Fernandina is the circumstantial accomplice of Andrés Ariza in a murder that occurs in her house. She lives in a prestigious neighborhood that borders a marginal one. The narrator finds this character and locates her in an affluent aristocratic part of the city. He describes Chulita as "the famous daughter of the Count of Talavera" (1003).[8] Then, he links Julia Fernandina to crime, her history, and other places that he considers important. The first suggests that she is the only woman in the neighborhood capable of being involved in the crime: "… [M]y imagination was boiling trying to reconstruct the history of the only woman of the neighborhood who could intervene in the crime …" (1004-5).[9] He does not find other women or men involved in the crime. Then, he addresses other places, such as Andalucía and her house. Although the story evokes the thought of civilization and barbarism,[10] it also gives a progressive fate to Chulita Ferna. In this sense, the gender tension in terms of male and female power is alleviated.

In Chulita Ferna's house, the novel presents the opposition of outside/inside to call attention to the aristocratic society. Her house is the place in which the criminal events have happened and in which three spaces are described as follows:

> … As I supposed the office and the bedchamber followed one after the other after the living room. There were only two high columns as a division between the alcove and the office. Behind them hung a splendid Brussels lace curtain made expressly [for her] no doubt because it bore Julita's monogram and her family's Count of Tolvanero crown.… [T]hen the bed appeared in white wood with remarkable carvings of golden roses and laces and pigeons, also veiled with lace and

---

[8] "…la famosa hija del conde de Talavera" (1003).

[9] "…hervía mi imaginación reconstruyendo la historia de la única mujer de la vecindad que podia haber intervenido en el crimen…" (1004-5).

[10] Isaac García-Guerrero in "Exhibición de Atrocidades: Andalucismo y Degeneración Racial Española en *Insolación* de Emilia Pardo Bazán" explains how Pardo Bazán not only was interested in racial theories at the time, but also, includes them in her works. García argues that Andalucía's culture in her novel *Insolación* represents racial degeneration that maintains the country in a setback state. *Insolación* was, as García points out, written after the Universal Exposition in Paris in 1889. Afterward, Pardo Bazán expressed a series of thoughts on Andalucian cultural representation and its link with Africa.

stuffed in silk ... It was there in that unspeakable place of gallantry and depravation where the victim had been sacrificed. (1006)[11]

The bedroom appears as a place of promiscuity that the narrator emphasizes to raise moral questions. These comments encourage the reader to see a decadent aristocracy and its sumptuous lifestyle. The house of Julia Fernandina (Chulita Ferna) is meant to present the cause of the crime. So, elements such as ordinary furniture and lack of ornaments, as the narrators point out, suggest the need for an economy of expenditure. The economic situation is the reason why Ariza kills the rich man in Chulita's house:

That damned Andrés! [He] was so bad about money; things got to such a point that they had no solutions.... He gambled, gambled and lost. He was desperate ... [B]ut look.... She opened a door adjoining the office and I saw a dismantled room with only a chair with uneven legs and a cheap table....
— That was the dining table.... [Chulita said] I had beautiful things.... Sculptures, wall hangings, embossed silver, carpets everything was gone.... One day he told me that we can get out of all this. (1008)[12]

The space here shows clearly the economic decay of Julia Fernandina and her lover. It helps to structure the character of Julia Fernandina in the crime scene and accentuates her emotional aspect. The reader infers that her attachment to Arisa is beyond economic reasons, whether the attachment has been emotional on her own, forced by him, or both. These three aspects explain why she engages in prostitution-like behavior in her house. She represents the aristocracy prostituted and, at the same time, lets the reader see how the aristocracy and high social class are involved in activities such as gambling. One of the elements that stands out is her shield of arms, which also enhances

---

[11] "... Como había supuesto el gabinete y la alcoba estaban seguidos, en pos de la sala. No dividían a la alcoba del gabinete sino dos altas columnas, detrás de las cuales colgaba una cortina de espléndido encaje de Bruselas, hecha expresamente sin duda pues ostentaba el monograma de Julita y la corona condal de la Tolvanero ... y apareció el lecho de madera blanca con tallas doradas admirables de rosas y carcajes y palomas, velado también de encajes mullido en cedas ... Era allí, en aquel nefando de galantería y depravación donde había sido sacrificada la víctima" (1006).

[12] "¡El malvado Andrés! Andaba tan mal de dinero; las cosas habían llegado a un punto tal, que no tenían solución ... El jugaba, jugaba y perdía. Se desesperaba. ... Pero mira ... Abrió una puerta contigua al gabinete y vi una habitación desmantelada con solo una silla paticoja y una mesa ordinarísima ...
— Eso era el comedor ... tenía preciosidades ... Tallas, tapices, plata repujada, alfombras. Todo marchó ... Un día me dijo que podíamos salir del paso; me dijo" (1008).

the notion of nobility's decline. It also serves to describe why this character has another chance and why she is free to go to France. In this sense, Pardo Bazán turns away from Naturalism's resolution of the problem in general, but from the Radical Naturalism perspective in particular, by letting the character continue with her life. Finally, the house allows crime and promiscuous sexual behavior out of the norm. Here, Pardo Bazán presents a scene with different tensions as they appear in Radical Naturalism. Chulita Ferna's fate is to leave and not die. Different from Radical Naturalism, writers from Spanish Naturalism carefully followed reality and considered the physical aspect as well as the spiritual aspect of the human being. It also tends to give special attention to the natural environment. Pardo Bazán's Naturalism also diverges from the Radical Naturalism scheme because it lacks determinism and sometimes appears hidden in her narratives (Barroso 30). Her novels and short stories with female characters have the New Woman traits.

La Peña in *La gota de sangre*

In Spain, nonetheless, from the early nineteenth century, the marriage between the family and the state brought to the fore a series of debates about brothels, prostitution, and its practices (Guereña 31). These debates continued throughout the *fin de siècle* to the beginning of the twentieth century (Bolea 74). The legal and social allegations coincide with the sociological and positivistic idea of the Spanish woman as a natural deviant (Tsuchiya 15). Nonetheless, in *La gota de sangre* questioning Julia Fernandina's social decay, the narrator not only makes assumptions about her sexual behavior but also links her to the place of origin, her house, and *la Peña* (the club).

The narrator provides a detailed description of the woman while, at the same time, he reconstructs Chulita Ferna's history and her roots:

> … From Andalucía? Yes … How had Julita, the daughter of a member of the high society become the Chula Ferna the star of gallantry? … She started with the youthful love, crazy, but sacred love, and ended in decadence and vice. By her twenties she scandalized the Andalusian's *high-life* (high society).[13] … [S]he escaped with her French teacher. In Paris the pigeons flew away. Horrors were told about the Parisian life of Chulita.… She came to Madrid and settled in luxury. None of the high society ladies addressed her anymore; but there were two or three others

---

[13] Emphasis from the source.

like her, fallen and expelled from the society, who attended her gatherings
in the company of many boys of the "crème de la crème." (1003)[14]

The narrator's reconstruction, based on rumors of Chulita's fall, is the first issue
the reader finds. For example, the narrator is not aware of how old she was
when she escaped to Paris. The novel also highlights Selva, the narrator, as a
character and as a creator of the story. He crudely unveils his own thoughts and
views to the reader. It is not only that he is an unreliable narrator, but he is also
a misogynist who gives opinions about mores from the male perspective. Selva
clearly shows his arrogance and his gender bias and provides the initial frame
for Chulita's deviant behavior through her place of origin, Andalucía. In this
sense, the narrator brings to the fore a pattern that appears in other writings of
Pardo Bazán: the juxtaposition between civilization and barbarism, or the
center-periphery binary (Filgueira 94), as mentioned above. That pattern is
clearly detailed early in the novel in his dialogue with Duran, who has many
linguistic idiosyncrasies that are delivered to the reader as a form of linguistic
deficiency. In addition, in his inquiry about the crime, Selva goes to the *Peña*
(the club) where he exposes the reader to a witness to Chulita's sexual behavior.

The *Peña* is a place owned by men. Women are absent here, but the erotic life
of women is the main topic of conversations in this place:

> I see myself at the Peña … Manolo Lanzafuerte and Pepito Arahal were
> talking about women, as usual. Their conversation was a mixture of
> cautious affairs of high society and noble ladies, with public cheatings
> prostitutes and mistresses; they gossiped about ruins, scandals,
> damages, noisy bells, and quiet intimidations. And the name of Chulita
> was mentioned. (1004)[15]

---

[14] "… ¿De Andalucía? Sí … ¿Cómo Julita, la hija de mejor sociedad se había convertido en
la Chula Ferna astro de la galantería equívoca? … empezando por el amor juvenil, loco,
pero sagrado, y acabando por el vicio y la decadencia.   A los ventitantos años,
escandalizando a la *high-life* andaluza … se fugaba con un maestro de francés. En Paris
abatieron vuelo los tórtolos. De la vida parisiense de Chulita se contaban horrores ….
vino a Madrid y se instaló con lujo. Ninguna señora la trató; pero hubo dos o tres, como
ella caídas y expulsadas de la sociedad que asistieron a sus tertulias en compañía de
'bastantes muchachos de la crema'" (1003).

[15] "Me veía en la Peña … Manolo Lanzafuerte y Pepito Arahal charlaban como siempre,
de mujerío. Mezclábanse allí los recatados deslices de altas damas y nobles dueñas con
las públicas aventuras de busconas y daifas; se recontaban ruinas, escándalos, daños
campanadas estrepitosas y mansos acoquinamientos. Y el nombre de Chulita salió a
relucir" (1004).

The space in this scenery represents not only a "*locus amoenus*" for men but also how patriarchy constructs women as weak and easily falling. These views are rooted in the idea of biological differences and the determinism of women in vogue during this time. Here, the social norm is policed by men, a nuance that has a biological origin according to Darwin and other scientific perspectives (Moi 16). Further conversations in this scene are not only about Chulita's sexual misconduct (e.g., involving money and dating old and rich men) but also about her eroticism. The *Peña,* then, is the place in which the construction of women as deviant is clearly open and literal. The narrator enhances these views later in Chulita's house by referring to her bedroom as a "terrible altar of gallantry and deprivation" (1009).[16] The novel portrays, in this way, her house as a brothel-like place, an evocative image that can be seen in other literary works. As the house in these novels has different heterotopic spaces, the countryside brings to the fore other possible misconduct. It is a relevant space in which many deviant behaviors will occur. While some of these stories present the house as the space in which women are allowed to engage in crimes, the countryside is totally dominated by male actions. It is a patriarchal ground. Female characters in these stories play mostly a passive role. This pattern appears in most of the novels mentioned above, while some female characters represent different deviations. In *La hija del bandido,* the landscape of rural Mexico enhances the vision of women through plants, topography, colors, and so forth. In this sense, it evokes a romantic narrative similar to Ignacio Manuel Altamirano's works.[17]

The Countryside and The House *Santa*

In Mexico, Gamboa's novel uses the countryside to deliver multiple representations, in particular in relation to the character of Santa. She plays an essential role because she connects the notion of the nation and Mexican women. The novel does so through the representation of the countryside of Mexico. The Mexican countryside, here, works as in la *hija,* though it is not clear to whom the land belongs. Nonetheless, as in the model of Radical Naturalism, the narrator suggests the negative traits of women. This suggestion happens when Santa escapes from her mother's supervision: "Other times with Augustina's permission, Santa used to go alone to the entrances of the Pedregal ..." (47).[18] The narrator translates Santa's thoughts about the Pedregal as a

---

[16] "... nefasto altar de galantería y deprabación" (1009).

[17] Ignacio Manuel Altamirano was the most notable writer in Mexico after independence. His writings engage the topic of nation-building. In many of his works the pastoral landscape is present to underline Mexican richness in natural resources and the beauty of the country. This is particularly emphasized in his major work *EL Zarco* (1901).

[18] "Otras veces y previo permiso de Augustina, Santa íbase sola hasta las entradas del Pedregal, un sitio maravilloso y único ..." (47).

wonderful place, but later he describes it as a dangerous site. He infuses irony in his tone when describing the Pedregal as

> Still unexplored …[,] immense, dotted with bushes and colossal monoliths, with declining stones, so slippery that not even the goats step on them … [, with] the herb that suspiciously hides; [the] deep and black dark caves, full of brambles, full of mystery, very deep chasms, very deep. (47)[19]

The Pedregal is an unexplored, virginal, and dangerous place full of mysterious peaks, declivities, slippery rocks, and deep, dark caves. Natural settings constantly connect geographic features with Santa's body to make contrasts between her rural pureness and her brothel life. For example, the slippery rocks suggest the idea that it is easy for a woman to slip with a man. These connections also assist the narrative in dissecting or constructing the female body and its desires throughout the novel (Castillo 179). In other words, this is a representation of a woman not only as a place but, more particularly, as a dangerous place. The use of visualization in the narrative also delineates the woman as mother nature, a motif that exposes the eroticism and fascination of the nineteenth-century man.

In fact, later in the narrative, after Santa falls (slips) for the alférez Marcelino Beltrán, the space metaphorically anticipates Santa's future, "– Give me your hand– says Santa–, don't look to the water … [H]alfway through that insecure trunk Santa stopped and with a solemn decision the abysm opened at her feet, the darkness of the night" (59).[20] These scenes sketch a degradation of the relationship between light and color that suggests that Santa will fall into the abyss. The narrative makes references suggesting that without a man who protects and provides economically for her, a woman will be in free fall. Also, the scene provides the idea of the danger that she faces as the space becomes black, dark, and with a deep abysm. Hence, as mentioned above, the reference evokes women as mysterious beings, difficult to understand, and dangerous. In contrast, Santa's story starts in a little white house in the countryside, suggesting purity and innocence. Additionally, the story not only links the place with Santa herself or her body but at the same time also depicts this female

---

[19] "Inexplorado todavía … inmenso, salpicado de arbustos monolitos colosales, de piedras en declive, tan lisas que ni las cabras se detienen en ellas … la yerba criminalmente disimula; cavernas y grutas profundas negras, llenas de zarzas, de misterio … simas muy hondas, hondísimas" (47).

[20] "– Dame la mano –repuso Santa–, no veas para el agua … A la mitad del inseguro tronco Santa se detuvo y, con una decisión más solemne el abismo abierto a sus pies, la obscuridad de la noche" (59).

character as naïve, innocent, uneducated, poor, and at the mercy of the natural elements (Ordiz 9). It is not difficult here to see how the novel conveys the idea that some spaces are dangerous while others are virginal. In both cases, the narrative links the landscape of the countryside with the woman's body. As in the Spanish novel *La prostituta*, the text emphasizes that women in nineteenth-century Mexican society are naïve and completely dependent on men. Moreover, the narrator comments on how women were expected to be accountable for their acts. During the last two decades of the nineteenth century, biology and other sciences reduced women to a series of diagnoses, a trend that went deep into the twentieth century, too. So, women needed to be guided by men in regard to any intellectual endeavor or with their understanding of right or wrong (Dijkstra 65). This pattern was used to control tightly all aspects of women's lives at the time. Gamboa's narrator avails himself of authoritative knowledge while making comparisons between the house and other spaces, such as the church, the city, the street, the restaurant, the countryside, or the little town. His main goal with these comparisons is to elevate his moral discourse. His comparisons happen throughout the novel when the narrator uses his language to express ideas about the characters. He not only poses as an authority in health and letters but also follows Zola's ideas. In this sense, the narrative also contributes to the process of social control. The narrator presents himself as a *letrado*[21] who shares the state's anxieties about cleanliness, health, and order, trends common in Mexico by the time of the *porfiriato*. The novel no doubt put Gamboa as part of the high social class from which he received monetary profits as an author, as Bourdieu suggests. These depictions of the rural space clearly picture the anxiety about control over women during the Victorian era. They are also present in the cultures of Latin America and Spain.

The Brothel in *Santa*

Another heterotopia in this social context is the brothel, a marginal space where crime is possible, along with other deviancies in women. As mentioned above and not an official brothel, according to the narrator, the house of Chulita Ferna is a place where she engages in prostitution-like behavior. The novel unveils the crime and lets the reader know how Julia Fernandina accomplishes it and how she gains redemption. In *Santa*, the brothel's violence and crime are intrinsically related when a murder happens inside:

---

[21] *Letrado*, in the context of Latin America, is a person who not only was educated, but also oversaw writing and reading legal documents. In general terms this person belonged to families of the middle or high classes.

The party kicked up, not worse than every other night; there were four or five individuals of decent appearance well known to the house,[22] who exuded a big and animated party spirit....
– It is true that you want trouble? – said the wise man being already unwise.... [T]he killer's movement, once started, proceeded by itself until the consummation of the assassination. Rodolfo faithfully cocked the revolver hammer. When the others tried to intervene, it was too late. (209-211)[23]

In this series of events, the brothel is the place that plays a central role related to criminal activity or simple violence (there are other instances of violence, too). In *La hija del bandido, La gota de sangre*, and Gamboa's novel, the female characters are surrounded by many transgressions in different ways, but they are not the ones who commit crimes. In *Santa*, the brothel highlights moral questions about the women and uses prostitution to frame crime, but it is a legal place. *La gota de sangre* allows a glimpse at some sort of prostitution, which involves crime. Both novels, *Santa* and *La gota de sangre* do not present prostitution as an illegal activity, though it is presented closely to the historical context of Mexico and Spain. In both countries, the exercise of prostitution was considered a form of deviance but not a crime.[24]

Prostitution was controversial from the early nineteenth century, and this trend did not change by the *fin de siècle*. Mexico's moral battles sparked by health anxieties were common while in the process of modernization of the *porfiriato* (Piccato 117-118). The state controlled prostitution during the late nineteenth and the early the twentieth century (Bliss 169). Spain regulated it from the mid-nineteenth century to the first half of twentieth century, but it

---

[22] *La casa* here refers to the business of the brothel.

[23] "La parranda se armó ni mejor ni peor que la de todas las noches; cuatro o cinco individuos de pergeño decente, conocidos de la casa[23] y que exudaban chispa sorda ...
–Decididamente quiere usted camorra? – declaró el juicioso sin mucho juicio ... el movimiento asesino que una vez comenzado empuja por sí mismo hasta la consumación del asesinato. Rodolfo, fatídico, amartilló el revólver. Cuando los demás pretendieron intervenir, era tarde" (208-211).

[24] In Mexico, as Katherine Elaine Bliss suggests, the legislature did not criminalize prostitution between 1876 and 1918, yet there were a series of modifications to the laws (see Bliss 169). In addition, as she points out, prostitution was the center of social discussion in regard to health and social order from the mid-nineteenth century to the mid-twentieth century. Similarly, in Spain, Jean Luis Gereña explains in "Historia de la prostitución en España siglos XIX y XX" that prostitution was constringed by a series of legal regulations but was not illegal. Hence, prostitution was constantly debated. In both countries allegations against prostitution based on the health concerns made it seen as a deviancy, but not as a crime.

was not punishable (Guereña 34). As with Spain and Mexico, England regulated it, though prostitutes were victims of police aggression (Walkowitz 23). In the United States, it was illegal, but with different nuances of the signifier "illegal" (Yamin 8). The legality of prostitution in the nineteenth century is in general, a chronological dispute. No doubt, it was historically present in these countries, allowing one to see how these narratives depict it from different perspectives. Although legal, prostitution had a heavy social and moral weight that was linked to women's sexuality.

Gamboa, for example, begins from the first chapter to point to the reader that the brothel is in a marginal neighborhood, or at least at the border of marginality. The place is full of plants in decay, a picture that contrasts with the pastoral view of the countryside, "[Santa] Almost without noticing that at her right was an anemic and unkept garden.... [, she] confusedly observed, something that looked like a lawn stunted and eroded away" (14).[25] The garden's disarray shows clearly that there is an intention to highlight the exterior not as a house but as a business. This visual scenery also evokes the dead flowers and their lack of life on the lawn as a reference to the women who settle in the brothel. Overall, it is a continual trope in the novel. The flowers are also used as a synecdoche for the fallen women. The scene represents Santa's future in the form of retrospective scenery.

These moral references and detrimental commentaries of the narrator are constant throughout the novel. As clearer later in the novel, the text explicitly links lesbianism as a vice with the brothel, "–Hipo! I cannot tolerate the Gaditana anymore. Imagine that she is convinced that I should love her more than any man.... [N]onetheless, she knew the meaning of Gaditana's outbursts. It was the old vice, the ancestral and teratologic vice that grows by preference in the brothel" (134).[26] While the narrator points out the brothel as the literal space in which lesbianism appears by "preference," his tone and the use of language simulates an opinionated authority. By echoing himself expressing that lesbianism is the vice, the ancestral vice, and overall, by referring to the teratology study, he positions himself as a scientific authority. The narrative targets the reader not from opinion but from the scientific argument that locates the brothel in a place where more than one sexual deviancy may occur. The narrator successfully claims a prestigious and prominent position as a very

---

[25] "Casi sin darse cuenta exacta de que a su derecha quedaba un jardín anémico y descuidado ... Sí advirtió confusamente, algo que semejaba césped raquítico y roído" (14).
[26] "–¡Hipo! ya no aguanto a la Gaditana. Figúrese usted que está empeñada en yo que la quiera más que cualquier hombre...no obstante, sabía el significado de los arranques de la Gaditana. Era el vicio antiguo, el vicio ancestral y teratológico que de preferencia crece en el prostíbulo" (134).

well-educated man, a *letrado*, a sort of special authority in the Latin American social context. These ideas converge with Foucault's arguments about the place of sexuality in the nineteenth century, in which the marriage bedroom was the unique place for expressing and practicing it, and how this rhetoric came from the biological sciences as an entity of control. Foucault's concept of heterotopia explains how and why Santa detaches from social control.

In Mexico City, the *porfiriato* tried to restructure the urban space, and it was redesigned in areas dominated by the state, the elite, and the poor, marginalized citizens, creating social conflicts and challenges for the designers. The modernization of health, cleanliness, order, and control of public spaces were priorities for Mexico City at the time. These developments conflicted with the "*old barrios*" that tended to be marginal and lacked basic public services such as sewage or running water (Piccato 117). All these details are reflected in the character of Santa. The narrator's voice itself reflects the conflict between marginal "*old barrios*," the brothels, and modernization. Between 1876 and 1898, heterotopic spaces such as the brothel in Mexico were legal and controlled by the state (Piccato 117). Gamboa's novel shows this particular aspect in great detail.

The brothel is a marginal space that historically presented struggle in Mexico City at the end of the nineteenth century. Gamboa's novels describe Santa's house and the brothel by means of comparison. Other elements mark the determinism of women and serve to frame depictions of their fall. In the novel, the main character's house is located in rural Mexico in the town of Chimalistac. This place suggests security and comfort, while the narrative uses pastoral elements to put a positive mark on the description. As the narrator states, "– there was a little white house, with an entrance of wood without carving. … The patio has the firmament for a ceiling and six orange trees full of fruits as ornaments" (40).[27] The house full of light and the white color alone have a polysemy because they make a series of references. For example, lightness and whiteness indicate virginity, purity, honesty, and other virtues. The flowers are delicate and easy to pull out from the plant. The reference to flowers is also earlier in the novel, "Her story ... of poor girls born in the countryside and raised outdoors in the flowers" (39).[28] The flowers represent the girls of rural Mexico and their youth, freshness, tenderness, and vulnerability. The fruit evokes fertility and abundance. So, the narrative's use of the fullness of fruit indicates the prosperity and richness of the rural town. It

---

[27] "– una casita blanca, de reja de madera sin labrar ... su patio con el firmamento por techo y por adorno hasta seis naranjos desgajándose en frutos" (40).

[28] "¡Su historia...! ... de las muchachas pobres que nacen en campo y se crían al aire libre entre brisas y flores" (39).

also represents Santa's character as a metaphor for the nation and its stagnation (Ordiz 14). Overall, this visual scenery of rural life is a national trope that reverberated from the early nineteenth century. It also appears in Atamirano's works. The wood that is not carved, mentioned by the narrator, points out the modesty of Santa's house while suggesting the simplicity of its inhabitants. This is a religious perspective that is common in Catholicism. The hidden aspect of the house gives the sensation of protection. By being expelled from her house in the form of expulsion from paradise, Santa is separated from the women's Mexican identity (e.g., Catholic and faithful to their husbands).

To enhance the sensation of protection, the narrator describes the room of Santa's brothers as follows, "In a corner, [there is] the shotgun … and a bag with bullets that can be used to hunt in the hills and for defense of the little house" (40).[29] The shotgun is the element that needs to be highlighted because it defends the house and protects Santa. In the interior of the house, everything is clean and orderly, and the narrator highlights that the mother sleeps with the daughter. This arrangement is another aspect of protection from Santa's possible sexual encounters with her brothers or other males. This trend is found in a nation-building context as a patriarchal act in which the older women are called to police the sexual behavior of younger women (Mayer 7). In other words, Santa's house provides an environment that is juxtaposed with the brothel. Then, *Santa* uses the house to frame the main character, Santa, who is surrounded by a series of positive elements and values. Later, her mother and brothers take this comfortable and secure situation away from her.

Nonetheless, another set of rules appears when Santa arrives at Pepa's house. This house is in disarray. It lacks organization, and the furniture is all over the place. In contrast, Santa's house is, at least at first sight, clean, safe, and comfortable. The house of Pepa, the madam, is described as follows:

> … [W]ith her she crossed two hallways and the dark and smelly dining room with two pallets as a carpet. …Then Santa crossed a corridor … [,] and at an angle of the stretched and very small courtyard, they continued and passed a door with blurry glass. (18)[30]

---

[29] "En un rincón, la escopeta … y una bolsa con los perdigones … que tanto sirven para cazar en el monte cuanto para defender la casita" (40).

[30] "… con ella cruzó dos pací[l]los obscuros y mal olientes, una sala con dos camastros por alfombra todavía… Luego atravesó Santa un corredor. … y en un ángulo del reducidísimo patio, pasaron frente a una puerta de vidrios apagados" (18).

Naturalist aesthetics often involves references to bad odors and darkness. She examines the Latin American naturalist discourse, looking at the brothel as a heterotopic space that frees and embraces women (Venegas 254). Nonetheless, the brothel and its physical boundaries are understood as a heterotopic space in which national, social decadence and corruption are reflected. This relationship between the house and the brothel gives the naturalist narrative a strong foundation for the female character's trajectory toward a deterministic fate. This treatment of the space also reinforces and refers to the lack of cleanliness as laziness, a creative way to use social Darwinism.

In contrast to the mother's house, the entrance to the brothel offers a stretched, dark, confusing space and other negative sensations to Santa. We find that while walking throughout the brothel, the visual opposes the virtues suggested in her house. Other elements, such as the "maid," have a heavy moral implication, though she is not a prostitute. Therefore, the novel raises a question about the determinism in the character of Santa, stating in between the lines that there are other works for Santa to perform. The reader clearly does not have access to Santa's thoughts, but it can be inferred that she has other alternatives. Nonetheless, the brothel welcomes Santa, and it gives her a better living. The brothel, as a heterotopic space, is presented throughout with views of calm and intimate places and states, similar to Santa's room in Chilamistac. The comparisons between the countryside's pastoral landscapes, Santa's house, Pepa's house, and the brothel allow the reader to see how the narrative constructs deviancies in the main character and in other characters. They also underline how Santa becomes the spectacle of punishment as a model that shows what could happen to a woman who crosses the patriarchal constraints. This trend demarks many characteristics attributed to Radical Naturalism. Nonetheless, in all these spaces the borderline of social class and the binary of normal-abnormal sexuality are not clearly delimited. Liminal spaces provide different possibilities to the characters to cross different borders.

Liminality

The border between many aspects of existence provides the material for the state of instability that must be reached by a rite of passage to go through the threshold. This peculiarity allows for the creating of individuals or characters who move across the social, political, and spiritual borderlines. In many of these scenarios, the transition creates a "limbo" or "limbic" state, a concept borrowed from Christianity in which the non-baptized were in the threshold between heaven and hell, waiting for resolution (Patterson 46). These aspects appear not only in marginal societies but also in other societies as they are culturally iterative[31]. In Hardy's novel, as mentioned above, the scene of The Flower-de-Luce offers clear examples of liminal spaces that intersect with other liminalities. This scene suggests a continual relationship between aristocratic men and rural women hidden in a marginal space that allows for precise liminality not only in the space but also in some characters. Tess seems to go through a rite-like passage. As mentioned, from the reader's perspective, she does not belong in this space. Other participants and Alec d'Urbervilles induce and present the scene to Tess, as when Alec explains to her how other women behave at these events, remarking "...They don't like to everybody see" (78) or when "a young man with a wet face" (78) approaches her to explain, "Don't ye be nervous" (78). In addition, Alec does not use Tess's name. Instead, he calls her "my Beauty" several times. Here, as in rites of passage, Tess's name is changed by Alec. It is very common to change the name of the subject that goes through the threshold (Patterson 55). In this case, changing the name allows liminality in the female characters that intervene in this particular excerpt. By their nickname or new name, they become visible and invisible in social contexts. For example, Nancy and her sister Card Darch are nicknamed Queen of Diamonds and Queen of Spades, respectively. Their nickname erases their social identities. Liminality not only serves to highlights deviancies, but also helps to frame crime in Tess. She has full access to The Herons Inn, and she obtains it under the name of d'Urbervilles. While this change of name gives her the power to enter an aristocratic inn, it also allows her to kill Alec. The Herons join Tess in the in-betweenness as a liminal space. Here, space plays a special role as it simultaneously facilitates interrelationships and their coexistence in their own social, political, gender, or philosophical order (Lefebvre 70). Nonetheless, the gathering referred to above facilitates instances of abuse, such as Tess's rape.

In *La gota de sangre*, the house located between two neighborhoods becomes a liminal element since it points out the boundary between good and bad areas. It is an instrument that helps one to understand the fall of the aristocracy when the crime is committed in Julia Fernandina's house located in a good neighborhood of the aristocratic community. This space also underlines the differences between crime and deviance. The narrator alerts the reader to the fall of Julia Fernandina, and he literally explains not only why she changes her name to Chulita Ferna but also how that change happens. She also becomes a liminal subject that no longer belongs to the aristocracy as the narrator points out, "None of the high society ladies addressed her anymore; but there were two or three others, like her, fallen and expelled from the society, who attended

---

[31] This term refers to iteration of cultural practices or narratives such as rites, epic poems and so forth.

her gatherings" (1005).[32] Chulita Ferna's appropriation of her own sexuality is not only taken as a sexual misconduct that is far from the norm but also allows her to circulate beyond the aristocratic social domain, as the quote suggests.

In *The Awakening,* the sea and the seashore create a borderline used by the narrative as the location of liminality. Together, these spaces are a barrier that Edna has to overcome in the last scene. This particular place, as Hong suggests, constitutes a patriarchal domain even regarding the artistic representation in which Edna wishes to participate. Art, for example, is another element that detaches Edna from the patriarchal domain (Hildebrand 200). Here, nonetheless, the sea becomes not only an allegory of male dominance but also a "female utopia" (Hong 89). It is also used by the siren's archetype as an erotic place in which the sirens belong to two worlds (Butkus, Fleury, and Raoulx 121). Depictions of sirens represent the male fear of "free" women who are autonomous (Dijkstra 265). Edna transgresses many social norms in these spaces, contributing to the questioning of patriarchy. In addition, Edna's relation to these spaces challenges the male dominance of the shores and the sea. For instance, when she learns how to swim, she claims both spaces. Edna then becomes an entity of two worlds, as the last part reveals, "The foamy wavelets curled up to her white feet and coiled like serpents about her ankles. She walked out. The water was chill, but she walked on. The water was deep, but she lifted her white body and reached out with a long sweeping stroke" (109). The story locates Edna in this position to subvert male dominance just before she dies. This is reiterated when she hears her father and her sister Margaret in a family-like scene. It is important to mention that Louisiana's laws at the end of the nineteenth century positioned the married woman as part of the husband's estate (Smith 512). Although Edna Pontellier does not change her name, she undoubtedly goes through something like a rite of passage when she awakes and changes: "Edna began to feel like one who awakens gradually out of a dream, a delicious, grotesque, impossible dream, to feel the realities pressing into her soul" (31). It is from here that the character starts to change her social and, ultimately, her sexual behavior outside of the social norm. She nonetheless claims her sexuality and the event of what it means to be a woman, as Toril Moi suggests. Additionally, Edna's suicide in the sea makes her into a siren who not only takes possession of a male-dominated space but also claims authority for herself. The liminal space here allows the character to own and liberate herself from the patriarchal dominance while she invades its owned space.

La hija presents to the reader a complex liminality in the space and in different characters, in particular María. Like *Tess,* the liminal space in *La hija*

---

[32] "Ninguna señora la trató; pero hubo dos o tres, como ella que caídas y expulsadas de la sociedad asistieron a sus tertulias" (1005).

goes beyond the cave and covers the rural geographical landscape and the town of Zapotlán. The rite of passage in the novel relates to Maria's transition from teenager to woman, in which she remains until the end of the novel while crossing different social and geographical spaces (LaGreca 75). Nonetheless, in this passage, María changes her name (from María Colombo to María Granados) in order to become a liminal character and move through all the spaces as the narrator shows in detail, "On the wide street of La Casita, at about eleven in the morning … [,] a carriage stopped … that should have taken about two or three days to travel the path. … A young lady, dressed with the elegance that suited her as a traveler, came down from the door" (38).[33] The description visually completes María's identity changes that she later unveils, "As my readers surmised, the travelers were none other than María Colombo and Juana" (39).[34] This change is critical for this character to resolve the problem of the novel while at the same time challenging the omnipresent patriarchal power projected by her father, Vicente Colombo. She is the antithesis of the Latin American nineteenth-century bandit. In other words, liminality in this novel brings to the fore the role of the woman. The novel's space not only interacts with the characters in a liminal way but also helps one to question the social, political, and gender aspects of the Mexican state.

Conclusion

To conclude, the house, the brothel, the cave, the inns, and the countryside play a vital role in these narratives. They provide a political, social, and gender framework for criminal or deviant female characters. In *Santa*, the space and liminality offer a contrast between the house and the brothel, implying a moral argument that questions crime and the practice of prostitution. Most important of all is that in the heterotopia of the brothel, crime is committed by men, but the focus of the narrative is always on Santa's character. The male characters involved in crime are not relevant in the story, while Santa's presence in the scene is overwhelming. This is an intentional strategy used to persuade the reader to have a negative view of the marginal places and of women. *La hija del bandido* offers a different view of women while it places the cave and countryside in prominence as a place of crime and deviancies. The cave is not only a variation of the house but also an antithesis of it. In this space, crime and deviancies triumph while the role of the woman is reduced to the daughter of

---

[33] "Por la calle ancha de la Casita, a eso de la once de la mañana … se detenía un coche … que debía haber hecho un camino de dos o tres días … Una dama joven, vestida con cierta elegancia que cuadraba bien a su calidad de viajera, bajó de la portezuela" (38).
[34] "Como mis lectores habrán adivinado, las viajeras no eran otras que María Colombo y Juana" (39).

a bandit. Nonetheless, these spaces frame the events and help María to reconstitute the universal order of the novel through heroism. She disrupts the father's omnipresent authority inside and outside the cave while she liberates the entire countryside and the town. In doing so, she does simultaneously display Catholic values and Mexican identity.

Across the Atlantic, in Pardo Bazán's *La gota de sangre*, deviance, crime, and liminality are enclosed in the spaces of the house and the neighborhood. The house is the place that delimits deviancy and sexual behavior. These elements highlight and unveil the female character Chulita Ferna. They show how she is emotionally attached to Ariza, the reason for her participation in the crime. It is in her house that the reader understands the story and how she becomes a liminal subject. On the other hand, the space of Chulita's house is on the threshold of the marginal limits, which question societal and aristocratic shallow appearances. In all these cases, the female character does not receive punishment directly. On the contrary, she is allowed to survive. *Tess of the D'Urbervilles* offers multiple scenarios of deviancies, crimes, and even heroism. The first occurs in the scene of The Flower-de-Luce, in which deviant sexual behavior not only happens but also allows for liminality in the space and characters. For example, the character of Nancy changes her name and actively participates in the event. The Herons scene questions the reader's perception, allowing catharsis and a sense of justice. These last two later disappear when Tess dies. These points need to be highlighted because the novel engages in questioning the rural society. From the perspective of Tess, a "pure woman," the reader questions the Victorian values framed in these places and events, which deviate from naturalistic schemes.

In Chopin's narrative, crime is not present, but Edna Pontellier is the personification of deviancies from the perspective of nineteenth-century society. The house facilitates the event of the awakening of Edna and weakens male power. She transforms herself in an event that is a rite-like occurrence. After the episode, her social entanglement becomes outside of the normal code. The seashore, the sea, and their borderline are liminal places in which the archetype of the sirens is present. To show Edna in the form of a siren is to create a representation of a strong woman who embodies danger in the space dominated by man. Here, the archetype works effectively when Edna invades a patriarchal domain. Special attention should be paid to patterns of the space used by Hardy, Barragán de Toscano, and Chopin. In their works, the patriarchal dominance is destroyed in the house or house-like spaces. Edna awakens in her house, claiming her freedom from her husband. In this case, the husband's authority is decimated by Edna's words. María destroys her father's banditry in the famous scene of the opium. She overpowers her father's omnipresent authority and power in order to revendicate herself. Last, in The

Herons, in a house-like space, Tess kills Alec and the narrative interacts with the reader's catharsis, producing a feeling of justice. The production of these characters, heterotopias, and agents of gender addresses the deviancies as a serious issue in all the novels. Some keep characters questioning patriarchy from the New Woman perspective, while characters tend to be associated with Victorian values or seen as agents of change. Yet, Radical Naturalism narratives allow one to ignore the question of patriarchy. The space, no doubt, plays a vital role in depicting deviancies and crime in these narratives. It is a good strategy to persuade, to underline, and to teach the reader other aspects of the characters. As space plays an important role in framing deviancies and crimes in female characters in the novels mentioned above, other important aspects of the novel, such as scientific perspectives in eugenics, were prominent for explanations of deviancies in women. In the next chapter, I address the themes of eugenics, social Darwinism, and deviancies embedded in the cultural reflections of *Santa* and *Tess of the D'Urbervilles*.

Chapter 3

Santa and Tess of the D'Urbervilles: Eugenics, Alcoholism, and Social Darwinism

By the mid-nineteenth century, Charles Darwin, in his work *The Origin of Species by Means of Natural Selection, or The Preservation of Favoured Races in the Struggle for Life* (1859), explained how organisms evolved due to environmental effects and how those effects led to what he called "differential reproduction" or natural selection (Berra 68-69). By the 1880s, Francis Galton had come up with the theory of "eugenics," in part based on Darwin's theory of evolution and Galton's own ideas about physical and psychological traits (Bulmer 79).[1] Another *fin de siècle* scientific development was criminal anthropology, a new science at the time based on the Darwinian biological theory. This scientific perspective not only dealt with criminality in general but also taxonomized the criminal man and the criminal woman. One of the most prominent figures of criminal anthropology was Caesar Lombroso, a positivist, who was considered one of the few scientists who paid attention to issues of criminality within psychiatry and/or psychology (Pirone i).

Lombroso, in his book *Criminal Woman, the Prostitute and the Normal Woman*, explored deeply crime in women. His work impacted the fields of medicine, psychiatry, and anthropology, as well as judicial systems, police, and urban normativity. His findings in criminal anthropology resonated all over the world (Rafter and Gibson 3-4). These three scientific perspectives, though not uncontested, influenced the late-nineteenth-century scientific conceptions, molded ideas about women, and appeared in social, historical, and political contexts. They delineated women's representations in literary works from Great Britain and Mexico. Gamboa's novel, *Santa*, shows a society that many times converges with Lombroso's and Galto's ideas. Hardy, considered a New Woman writer, depicts a society that similarly embraces the same ideas.

Thus, this chapter explores how Federico Gamboa's *Santa* (1903) and Thomas Hardy's *Tess of the D'Urbervilles: A Pure Woman* (1891) reacted in the form of a

---

[1] Although Galton is recognized for his eugenic theory, this line of thought has an earlier start in Plato's *The Republic* (Galton and Galton 99).

dialogue with the sciences of Cesare Lombroso's criminal anthropology and Francis Galton's eugenics and how cultural and social practices such as social Darwinism and alcohol consumption converge or diverge in the Mexican or British context in the literary portraits of female characters.

Definitions

Before discussing at length the depictions of female characters such as Tess and Santa, it is worthwhile to mention that the term atavism, related to the individual history, ancestral evolutive breaks, physical and psychological retrogressions, sexual deviations, or animalization of the human being (Seitler 2-5). It also referred to an evolutionary regression with racial connotations. As a theory, it provided the fundamental thoughts for eugenics practice (Siltler 5). Galton defined eugenics as:

> the science of improving stock, which is by no means confined to questions of judicious mating, but which especially in the case of man, takes cognisance of all influences that tend in however remote a degree to give to the more suitable races or strain of blood a better chance of prevailing speedily over the less suitable than they otherwise would had. (Galton, *Essays in Eugenics* 25)

In other words, Galton adapted Darwin's theory of natural selection and applied it to the idea of race among human beings. "Social Darwinism" refers to the importation of Darwin's theory into social contexts. It is a term coined by Herbert Spencer to stigmatize and negatively stratify biological, social, and psychological "anomalies." The social Darwinism angle locates the poor or lower social classes as people with fewer possibilities of social, economic, and even biological progress. The use of this concept exploded rapidly in many societies around the world during the nineteenth century (Lewis 155). The term was also widely used in Latin American society, particularly in Mexico (Horcasitas 100). For example, the idea of social Darwinism appeared right after Darwin's works on evolution were published, and the term became formally used by Vicente Riva Palacio in the late 1880s. Palacio worked on applying Darwin's ideas to race and human differences (Delgado-Fernández 2). Social Darwinism, also, relegated the female to an inferior social status. According to Spencer, education would harm women psychologically (Richardson 40). The development of social and biological sciences suggests that in the nineteenth century these disciplines elaborated ways to control the individual. Michel Foucault explains the term "bio-power" as follows: "… one would have to speak of *bio-power* to designate what brought life and its mechanisms into the realm of explicit calculations and made knowledge-power an agent of transformation of human life" ("Bio-Power" 265; emphasis in original). Similarly, he suggests that discourse can be a series of procedures that deliver control, organization, and distribution of power to direct or redirect the expectations of a society. So, discourse is a mechanism of control delivered by different means and media. For example, control of sexuality by criminalization or penalization of homosexuality (Foucault, "The Order of Discourse." 52). The concept of atavism(s) is intrinsically linked to Naturalism. Both discourses conflate social and biological theories as an explanation for the human being.

Framework

As mentioned, Radical Naturalism used the experimental method of the scientific approach to depict society and frame characters. The core idea suggested is that writers need to discuss their works with marginal individuals and their role in society as a whole. Radical Naturalism's aim of writing is to examine society's problems from a scientific perspective. Such guidance changed the writings and the fate of the character(s) and social representations toward deterministic outcomes in the narrative worlds. Cesare Lombroso, a dedicated positivist, and Darwinist, studied women in the context of criminology. He argued that women become sedentary because of the demands that they take care of the children. He expanded the concept of atavism into a mechanism that regressed the individual into earlier evolutionary stages (Rafter and Gibson 7). In his work, he looked specifically at women as a prominent object of study (Tsuchiya 6) with tendencies toward social and biological regression: "...atavistically she is nearer to her primitive origin than the male..." (Lombroso, "The Insane Criminal: Special Forms of Criminal Insanity, Alcoholism" 107). Similarly, Isabel Clúa points out that the body of the famous female became a model of the eroticized object that transcended social boundaries while the famous female dancers and performers gained socioeconomic ground in late nineteenth-century Spain. Francis Galton, in his works *Hereditary Genius* (1869), *Inquiries into Human Faculty and Its Development* (1883), and *Essays on Eugenics* (1909), studies the variety of distinct capabilities of men "from different families and races" (Galton *Inquiries into Human Faculty and Its Development* 1). Galton's goal was to replace the good "stock" of the human capital of England and thus improve the nation's race. All these views constituted a point of departure in the fields of medicine, anthropology, and/or criminology (Tsuchiya 6). It is worth reiterating that the term of "bio-power" illustrates how, in the late nineteenth century, the body and sexuality were controlled not only biologically, medically, socially, politically, and psychologically, but also economically in engagement with capitalism. In his illustrative points, Foucault suggests that one of the important aspects of power is the use of biological fear in individuals, which allows the state or another authority to control or suppress sexuality and other aspects of human beings. Also, he explains how discourses are designed to control, regulate, or normalize society by different means and media. From a broader perspective of power, Edward Said notices that the hegemonic power of the French and British empires is "to be found already present in those very territories that are later to become formally central during the heyday of imperialist ideology. India, North Africa, the Caribbean, Central and South America... are sites of contention well before 1870..." ("Orientalism" 70). Hegemonic influences in Central and South America not only came from France and England but also from the United States at the end of the nineteenth century and at the beginning of the twentieth century. Yet, in Latin America, the process of nation-building occurred concomitantly with foreign powers such as the British Empire or the United States, which exerted control on the region. The United States Monroe Doctrine is one of the best examples of pressure on Latin America by foreign powers. This doctrine, made by President James Monroe in 1823, expresses that the "Western Hemisphere was no longer open to European colonization" (Sexton 3). The idea of the Monroe Doctrine's embedded language was to control European countries and especially to control Latin America's politics. Moreover, such a doctrine was useful for the United States' dominance in Latin American nations, particularly in the twentieth century (Sexton 6).

Likewise, Tamar Mayer points out that the nation-building process was a "hetero-male project" that left women relegated to the mere representation of the nation. This observation is valid for European countries (e.g., Spain or France) and Latin American countries. Furthermore, Pierre Bourdieu suggests that the artistic product (e.g., novels, paintings, and so forth) can be located in the field of power as elements that empower authors on a capitalist and economic basis. That is to say that during the *fin de siècle*, authors, intellectuals, and publishers became part of the field of power whenever they were subjects to be located as part of the dominant class. Recently, Paul Giles showed how an active discussion about the paradoxical posture of the United States culture in front of the British and their critical view permits a review from the Transatlantic perspective. This revision shows how Transatlantic studies allow one to constantly update the cultural discrepancies (Giles 21). Additionally, the "Cultural Studies" field was widened to view texts from a variety of disciplines, such as anthropology, sociology, media studies, and history, to name a few (Leitch and Lewis 225). The perspective of cultural studies helps one to understand the unbalanced power and manipulation of science in female portrayals as individuals in decadence in the late nineteenth and early twentieth century's international landscape across the Atlantic. These stances underline the depictions of the decline and possible backwardness of poor, lower-class, and aristocratic individuals. Literary works of the *fin de siècle* era negotiated social perception while maintaining an active dialogue regarding the dynamics of women in society. In this chapter's analysis, these theoretical formulations guide the aforementioned texts, and, at the same time, they illustrate how and why the cultural, historical, or social reflections appear in these novels. In many literary works, depictions of female characters express the nineteenth-century's concerns about eugenics and criminal anthropology. Authors such as Federico Gamboa or Thomas Hardy incorporated these perceptions and the opposition of gendered discourses, which are mirrored in the novels. The following paragraphs will review essays and other important literature relevant to the topics mentioned in the novels of *Tess* and *Santa*.

Criticism

Nicole Hahn Rafter and Mary Gibson explain the impact of the work of Lombroso and Ferrero in the nineteenth century and the early twentieth century. These editors provide a context for the reader to better understand certain aspects of criminal anthropology. For example, in the section "Atavisms and Prostitutes," they present the context in which Lombroso finds his own definition of "atavism" widely used in his work. *Santa* has been studied by Debra A. Castillo, Javier Ordiz, and Deborah Toner. They analyze the novel from different points of view. Castillo studies the novel from the perspective of the fallen woman and this figure's implications for women's sexuality. She pays special attention to the masculine narrative aesthetics of the *fin de siècle* and analyzes the text from a feminist point of view. These scholars greatly illuminate the Mexican context, while with the exception of Castillo, they do not at all address in any way the British context. Hence, Castillo gives a reinterpretation of the text based on the gender dialogues in the novel and makes an important but slight comparison between Gamboa's Radical Naturalism and Victorian literary works. She concludes that Gamboa's novel gives a broader vision of women's sexuality, which opens other possible perspectives through which to interpret the novel.

Javier Ordiz explores how the moral lesson and its content becomes a major literary product of the nineteenth-century narrative. He describes the character of Santa as a mirror of a moral value and as the state's representation of the woman in a complicated society at the *fin de siècle*. Ordiz renders an interpretation based on the sociopolitical accounts at the beginning of the twentieth century in Mexico. Deborah Toner examines Gamboa's novel in the context of Mexican nation-building at the *fin de siècle*. She comparatively studies the problem of alcohol not only in Gamboa's novel but also in other novels of the time. These three works address different aspects of the topics and themes of this chapter, and they greatly illuminate them in the context of Mexico, opening a Transatlantic window to discuss them. Pablo Piccato explains how the state, municipalities, and society raised anxiety about beggars, vagrants, and other socially marginalized people in Mexico at the turn of the century. Beatris Urías Horcasitas discusses the way in which social Darwinism was received and later established in Mexico at the end of the nineteenth century and how it was embedded in the state's politics and scientific thought.

Hardy's *Tess* has sustained literary criticism to this day. Angelique Richardson offers a plenitude of supplementary information about social Darwinism, alcohol, atavism, and other specifics of the novel in discussion here. In addition, the book addresses in great detail the Victorian thought on race and "eugenics" as sources of perception of Victorian writers, including the New Woman. Rosanna Nunan shows the novel's questions about heredity in the rural-urban opposition. She explores the topic of depictions of racial purity and shows how Hardy's novel uses the concept of eugenics to depict Victorian thought and its racial fears. Nunan examines the positivist thought from the perspective of the character of Angel and how these thoughts on the purity of women relate to Tess. Sara Beliveau compares the naturalistic structure of Zola and English literature. She suggests changes in regard to the main character's fate and shows how the narrative entangles gender, eugenics, and culture, particularly in Hardy's novel. Jane Lilienfeld discusses the prominent value that Hardy gives to social problems such as alcohol and health in Wessex. Although the chapter does not entirely focus on *Tess*, it addresses Victorian alcoholism from Hardy's perspective. Finally, Norbert Lennartz compares drunk characters in Dickens and Thomas Hardy's novels. He establishes how economic and spiritual aspects of the Victorian perception of the world are addressed differently by these authors. Nicole Lyn Lawrence examines how first-wave feminism used eugenics in its discourse, favoring the woman's health and life. The essay of Lara Marks shows historical statistical data and clinical records of women in pregnancy and childbirth in late nineteenth-century England. Finally, Roy Miller writes about the multiple relations that Great Britain had with Latin America in general. The book addresses the general overview of the diplomatic and economic relations between the British Empire and Mexico. This British and Mexican historical context, without a doubt, becomes necessary to analytically discuss the novels of Hardy and Gamboa in the following paragraphs.

Eugenics, Atavisms and Social Darwinism in *Tess* and *Santa*

In *Tess of the D'Urbervilles*, the ideas of eugenics and the criminal woman appear several times, and the novel, voluntarily or involuntarily, contradicts Lombroso's and Galton's ideas. Hardy's narrative presents a social landscape in which Francis Galton's studies of hereditary traits from the family can be referenced. In addition, the novel extends these premises to a gender dimension, giving an important place to women.

The text certainly shows how Tess's parents are in decay while she is depicted as healthy and strong. This evidence appears early in the novel when the reader notices the family dynamics among Tess, her father, and her mother. All of this happens after her father discovers his connection with the aristocracy. The narrator presents the character John Durbeyfield, Tess's father, as "... what was locally called a slack-twisted fellow; he had good strength to work at times; but the times could not be relied on to coincide with the hours of requirement ..." (39). Then the narrative highlights differences between Tess and her own family: "Tess meanwhile, ... was silently wondering what she could do to help them [her parents] out of it [their quagmire] ..." (39). These statements contradict the ideas of Galton, as he in his essay "The Possible Improvement of the Human Breed Under Existing Conditions of Law and Sentiment" asserts:

> In each class of society there is strong tendency to intermarriage, which produces a marked effect in the richness of brain power of the more cultured families. It produces a still more marked effect of another kind at the lowest step of the social scale. ... "Their life is the life of savages, with vicissitudes of extreme hardship and occasional excess" (19)[2]

Hardy's novel does not present this pattern. Moreover, later, the novel reveals Tess's tenacious character for hard work and resilience. There is no indication in the novel that Tess is in decay or that she has inherited decadent traits. She, in other words, has not inherited her father's lack of character, which the narrator unveils through the expression "slack-twisted fellow." The expression becomes ironic when it is followed by "he had good strength to work at times" (39). The story of Tess's family does not depict Galton's idea of heritage, which he suggests here: "When both parents are of the V class the quality of parentages is greatly superior to those in which only one parent is a V.[3] In that case the regression of the genetic center goes twice as far back towards

---

[2] Galton attributes the quoted portion to Charles Booth.

[3] V is one of Galton's classifications, as he explains in his essay "The Possible Improvement of the Human Breed Under Existing Conditions of Law and Sentiment" from his book *Essays on Eugenics* (1909) as he states: "The M in the upper line [of the table under discussion] occupies the position of Mediocrity, or that of the average of what all have received: the + 1°, + 2°, etc., and the - 1°, - 2°, etc., refer to normal talents .... As it will be useful henceforth to distinguish these classes I have used the *capital* or large letters R, S, T, U, V, for those above mediocrity and corresponding *italic* or small letters, *r, s, t, u, v,* for those below mediocrity, *r* being the counter part of R, *s* of S, and so on" (6; emphasis in original).

mediocrity ..." (18). The novel, then, emphasizes John Durbeyfield's slackness, while raising questions about gender and hereditary traits. It also questions the role of the Victorian man in rural settings.

Contrary to the male model, Tess and other female characters work hard in the country while accepting their condition. For example, Tess is more productive than Alec, Angel, and her father. Hardy, it is worthwhile to mention, did not recognize Galton's theory of eugenics; rather, he followed John Stuart Mill, who opposed it too (Richardson 44). Moreover, in Hardy's work, there is not a clear determinism like that in *Santa*. Tess is not expelled from her house; she decides to go and work in several lower-class jobs. In contrast, Santa is expelled from her house, and from that moment, her life starts to deteriorate.

The text also differs from the idea of the sedentary woman as a form of atavism. Under such a perspective, the tendency toward sedentarism in women leads to a certain form of criminal behavior, namely prostitution. Certainly, Tess does not show any kind of deviant behavior. On the contrary, she decides to help her parents economically, and she goes to work in different hard jobs. The character does not align with the idea of atavism as an individual regression to a primitive or savage. Tess is different from characters of Radical Naturalism, such as those in *La prostitute* or in *Santa*, who do not find a job and thus are left with the only choice of prostitution.

In the depiction of Tess's family, the novel sparks visions of domesticity that fade out while depicting the Victorian man as a diminished provider. She cannot be taxonomized under Lombroso's "types" of women: the prostitute, the criminal, the normal female, the female lunatic, and the Papuans, as she does not show any inclination toward them. It is important to highlight that Lombroso is not entirely clear about what constitutes a prostitute since many times he refers to them as criminal woman. Nonetheless, from his perspective, all poor women are prone to prostitution (Rafter and Gibson 10).[4]

Tess's psychological and moral states during the novel are a continuum of honesty, decency, and innocence. She, as the title of the novel suggests, is a "pure woman," and many times, she does not understand her evil social surroundings. The narrator explains that "... she was a fine and picturesque country girl, and no more" (14). In Hardy's narrative, the social class in rural settings emulates the urban one (Boumelha 131). Alec and his mother represent the top of the social strata as the richest families that became aristocracy, Angel and his family the middle-class, and finally, Tess and other

---

[4] Lombroso suggests also that women from upper classes can become prostitutes and draws a distinction between prostitutes and occasional prostitutes (Rafter and Gibson 219-220).

country women the working class. Tess belongs to the lower classes, but she does not engage in prostitution or other deviancies by her own initiative, as Lombroso predicts.

In addition, the novel inscribes Tess with traits of Anglo-Saxon superiority and makes comparisons based on gender. The treatment of the character of Tess in the novels reveals that she is a very strong woman and how she overcomes adversity. Another example is a comparison between Tess and her father that represents a polarized view of the male and female roles in Victorian society. This contrast is constant throughout the novel, and it becomes clearer as the novel moves forward when Tess engages in relationships with other men. She can be compared with Alec and Angel, a comparison in which she shows outstanding and better social and moral behavior than these men. Furthermore, the novel refers to barbarism while describing Alec:

> He had an almost swarthy complexion, with full lips, badly moulded, though red and smooth, above which was a well-groomed black moustache with curled points, though his age could not be more than three- or four-and-twenty. Despite the touches of barbarism in his contours, there was a singular force in the gentleman's face, and in his bold rolling eye (44).

By inscribing barbaric physical traits to this character, the narrative undermines Alec's heritage. It is a racial and social commentary to portray and highlight Alec and his family's bad behaviors with women. These descriptions contrast with how the narrator refers to Tess. It is very common to see references such as "beautiful feminine tissue," "sensitive," "blank as snow," and so forth. Overall, these comparisons highlight the importance of Tess as a role model for women.

Nonetheless, while presenting Tess as a model of Anglo-Saxon superiority, the narrative not only undermines patriarchal dominance but also gives women a great deal of visibility in England's rural context.[5] It is significant, that in Hardy's novel, the woman's body appears to partially represent Edmond Demolins's values. He suggests that the English woman is attached to the countryside and has knowledge of her duties, contrasting the French or Latin woman, who is not inclined toward farm work (Demolins 123). In fact, the story highlights the contrast between Tess and her Middle Ages ancestors: "Doubtless some of Tess

---

[5] Edmond Demolins in his book *Anglo-Saxon Superiority: To What It Is Due*, attributes the superiority of the Saxons in Wessex, Essex, and Sussex to the birth in a geographical condition that led them to progress from farmers attachment to the soil, to manage organization of the land, to independence.

d'Urberville's mailed ancestors rollicking home from a fray had dealt the same measure [as Alec] even more ruthlessly towards peasant girls ..." (91). This excerpt examines the feudal society in which feudal lords "owned" all aspects of the peasantry, including young women. It marks the lack of differences between the Victorian aristocracy or rich families in rural society and those feudal practices, pointing to political stagnation with no changes in male dominance. The excerpt also refers to the city dwellers as a depraved population. The city of London was the subject of tense eugenics discussions in the context of the upper social class's concerns about the reproductive tendencies of the poor and sexual encounters between social classes (Richardson 13). Additionally, Angel has no respect for rural women; this could be why Angel leaves Tess without a word.

The novel, nonetheless, offers a multiplicity of interpretations and connections between social classes, so readers' views of Tess might vary, as Hardy suggests in "The Profitable Reading of Fiction":

> ... a young and ingenious, though not very profound, critic ... propounded that novels in which depict life in the upper walks of society must ... be better reading than those which exhibit the life of any lower class. ... At the first blush this was a plausible theory; but when practically tested it is found to be based on such a totally erroneous conception ... as to not be worth a moment's consideration. (123)

Tess includes rural scenery, and in the social landscape, the Victorian aristocracy is located at the top of social strata. Hardy's narrative discusses a link between Tess and her aristocratic lineage. For example, Tess's father knows about his ancestors, "Your ancestor was one of the twelve knights who assisted the Lord of Estremavilla in Normandy in his conquest of Glamorganshire" (4). This can be understood as a military reference that contrasts with the view of John Durbeyfield as a "slack-twisted fellow." The excerpt confirms Tess's character as she goes through tough times later in the novel. She shows that she has not only discipline but also courage and endurance. One character affected by some kind of regression is Tess's father, who also can be seen as a degenerated individual of the working class. The reader sees how John Durbeyfield does not improve his social or economic situation. He is lazy, drinks heavily, and immerses himself in cottage life. The interpretations of the novel from different perspectives encourage the reader to understand that men, as well as women, can be depraved and fall. They also suggest an argumentative commentary about the scientific views of gender at the *fin de siècle*, and they contribute to the understanding of the means through which the social and biological sciences operated at the time. The presence of all these nineteenth-century sciences in literary works across the Atlantic Basin are good examples of bio-power. Different scientific works designed methods and taxonomies of the classification of individuals, which then led to transformations in many ways. These works became a discourse through which daily life was interpreted and acted on by the late nineteenth century. A good example of bio-power methods and taxonomies as a form of control can be found in Francis Galton's work.[6] Galton's discourse was strong, and many New Woman writers of the time actively engaged with his ideas. In the midst of the turn of the century, the prominent British author Sarah Grand, along with others, supported the idea of women as less disposed to have amoral sexuality. Additionally, in her view, women were entitled to rationally find a better partner for reproduction (Lawrence 373-374). In her short story "The Wrong Road," Grand creates a main character who suffers because she has lost the man of her dreams, but the story ends with her content at having lost him. This is a good example of Grand's depictions of women's autonomy, particularly in regard to finding a partner. Thomas Hardy's worries focused on rural life. As we see in the novel, his main concerns were the problems that rural people went through and why they relocated themselves to the cities, mostly London (Richardson 18). In this context, Nunan references Alec in relation to the perspective of Demolins, in which the rural immigrant to the town or city has already tainted and will continue to deteriorate the race. The position of Hardy in relation to Grand as New Woman authors is, to some extent, ambiguous. Nonetheless, he deconstructs eugenics in the novel.

Similar to inherited traits, physical qualities, sickness, bodily anomalies, or any other noticeable change in the body were problematic and could be considered signs of atavism or backward eugenics (Seitler 7). These ideas of eugenics and atavism in the *fin de siècle* served to legitimize policing the moral and medical role of the human body in society (Seitler 6-7). Hardy's novel questions the social spectrum, underlining marginal demarcations in which the aristocracy at the top of the social structure plays a vital role in balancing the social strata.[7] The story, in fact, creates a shadow of doubt about Alec's good

---

[6] As David J. Galton and Clare J. Galton show in their essay "Francis Galton: And Eugenics Today: *"Worth [was] estimated either by class place or by scale of value..."* (100). These authors also highlight different consequences of Galton's applied ideas and their negative and positive impact in England and elsewhere (Galton and Galton 102). As these authors suggest, Galton's aim was to improve the national race, resulting in Galton's proposal for the creation of the national eugenic record by taxonomizing families by their "worth." He designed the "Eugenic Certificate," which collected English families information containing items such as "Name," "Sex," "Age of death [if deceased]," "Cause of death [if deceased]," and so forth. The objective was to determine where these families or applicants where suitable and what could be considered inherited improvements.

[7] In this context, Galton's theory of taxonomized families according their worth from "gifted" to "degenerated," with "capable" and "average" in between (Galton and Galton 101).

hereditary stock when the narrative contrasts him with Tess. This doubt appears clearer in the novel at the time of the death of Tess's child, Sorrow:

> The infant's breathing grew more difficult and the mother's mental tension increased ...
> [S]he took the baby from her bed – a child's child — so immature ...
> So passed away Sorrow the Undesired – that intrusive creature, that bastard gift of shameless Nature who respects not the social law; a waif to whom eternal Time had been a matter of days ... (118-121)

The omnipresent narrator not only explains the child's medical problems visible to all, but also refers to the mores behind the baby's birth and death. He adopts the voice of the social discourse that controls and polices sexuality when he uses derogatory terms such as "bastard" or "shameless." In addition, the narrator raises social questions when he uses the word "undesired" in reference to Sorrow. For example, he raises the question, for whom was the child undesired? It is not the mother who rejects the child: "the mother's mental tension increased. It was useless to devour the little thing with kisses ..." (118). She seems to cope with the child's undesirability before the narrator tells the reader. The description makes clear that it is Alec and the rest of society who do not want this baby. Nonetheless, poor conditions might have played a role in children's demise, particularly in the countryside (Marks 519). The rate of women giving birth under poor conditions by the late nineteenth century was particularly high (Marks 520). From the scientific perspective, women were a subject of interest. [8] Nonetheless, the figure of the woman was erased from the family history; women did not represent value in any sense. Hardy's novel offers a different perspective; the novel provides a clear view of the woman's line in the episode of Sorrow.

The novel presents the event of Sorrow's death in two ways. On the one hand, it attributes death to the environment of the countryside, while on the other hand, it attributes it to the child's hereditary weakness. However, that weakness does not appear to have been inherited directly from Tess. By the turn of the twentieth century, several positivist studies of hereditary traits had been carried out. They focused on hereditary deviancies and found a correlation between deviancies and the ancestors of the studied individuals. In other

---

[8] Galton in his book *The Hereditary Genius* (1869) suggest that woman's hereditary line add little in regard to "judicial ability" (63). He also finds that the female influence is lesser in the transmission of inheritance for kinship of a second degree of familiarity, and he finds it difficult to conduct statistical analysis of third-degree relation due to the fact that the female biographical accounts were not recorded.

words, in the context of *fin de siècle* thinking, the case of the death of Tess's child could be explained by any environmental conditions or by a hereditary condition. Regarding the latter, Tess does not show that kind of weakness. The baby's weakness most certainly would have come from the father, Alec, or from Tess's father, who has heart problems, as Fincham suggests. Angel's father reinforces this view:

> Mr. Clare the elder ... went on with the story he had been about to relate; which was that after the death of the senior so-called d'Urberville, the young man developed the most culpable passions, though he had a blind mother, whose condition should have made him know better. (213)

So, the story establishes this significant biological precedent that makes the reader understand Sorrow's hereditary problems. It is a direct reference to syphilis and to the aristocrat Alec as the porter of the disease. The child's death by health complications also calls into question his inherited traits. More important, in Galton's taxonomy of families, Tess's case has no place. Could one consider Tess's family as capable? Or as gifted? It is difficult to provide an exact answer for these taxonomies. On the other hand, Alec is an educated person, but his rich family[9] is contaminated with syphilis. As an allegory, this event shows opposition to the idea of country women as eugenically pure because the product of men from upper social strata corrupts with sickness the purity of the country women. So, the novel here presents a challenge regarding different taxonomies used at the time. It creates a contradiction in the sciences of genetics, in which the woman's line has less probability of inheritance. It no doubt points to the high social strata's biological contamination. This assertion can be connected to how the novel uses a high social class to represent degeneracy. Hardy outlines a world in which Tess's depictions of atavism are not the views of the woman from the natural sciences at the *fin de siècle*. Instead, his novel features and portrays rural women as victims of other social classes (aristocratic, rich, middle, and lower classes). Although Hardy works the naturalistic scheme into this novel very well, he does not imprint Tess with deviant behavior. Moreover, as the novel progresses, it reveals Tess's physical, moral, social, and ethical strength. In this respect, she exceeds all the male characters. Throughout, Hardy underlines inherited traits in the main character, who is the idea of a pure woman in Victorian rural society. By presenting all these aspects of Tess, the narrative suggests that a strong woman does not need a male figure, a message very characteristic of the New Woman perspective. It was a controversial and, to some extent, anti-establishment perspective that resonated a great deal across the

---

[9] Alec family pretends to be aristocratic, but they are not.

Atlantic, but mostly in the United States. In Latin America, nonetheless, Radical Naturalism was a perspective with a great deal of diffusion that took advantage of marginal female depictions.

Before continuing with the contrast with *Santa,* it is important to provide a historical background of the relationship between England, Latin America, and Mexico. The British Empire influenced Latin American and Caribbean regions in different ways, as Edward Said states.[10] The economy was the main interest of the British Empire in Latin America in the early nineteenth century, when England promoted intense diplomatic relations along South America, Central America, and the Caribbean (R. Miller 38). Nonetheless, these relations tended to decline by the end of the nineteenth century as the Latin American countries engaged in a series of civil wars that disrupted British investments. Thus, "Commanders had instructions not to interfere in local politics, but they were also expected to follow diplomats' instructions and to defend British lives and property" (R. Miller 59). Great Britain interpreted the constant unrest of Latin American countries as uncivilized behavior and categorized them as semi-barbaric nations. This categorization was another aspect of the social Darwinism practiced across the Atlantic. Mexico and Great Britain engaged in what Paul Garner calls the "*imperialismo informal*" [informal imperialism], in which the relations between the countries were strictly economic, and only companies and financial entities were involved. As Garner suggests, the British interest was merely economic and had no other value. The British Empire did not engage in social progress, scientific trade, or even artistic contributions. Debra Castillo brings to light a valuable but slight comparison between Victorian literature and Federico Gamboa's Radical Naturalism. Castillo refers to Gamboa and his work on the prostitute as an inauthentic writing from the perspective of Naturalism. Contrasting Gamboa's work, the New Woman writers not only focused on stories that came from reality but also took advantage of certain themes to educate the reader (Richardson 86). Although Gamboa's novel could have a great deal of inherited traits from different positions, many are related to the concept of marginal societies.

---

[10] Edward Said in his essay "Yeats and Decolonization" points out, "One of the salient traits of modern imperialism is that in most places it set out quite consciously to modernize, develop, instruct, and civilize the natives ... The annals of schools, missions, universities [,] scholarly societies, hospitals in Asia, Africa, Latin America, Europe, and America fill its pages, and have had the effect over time of establishing the so-called modernizing trends in the colonial regions..." (74-75) According to Said's commentary the ideas of eugenics and criminal anthropology were brought to Latin America. Thus, these ideas were to some extent subject to different interpretations.

Santa addresses the concepts of eugenics, atavism, and Social Darwinism inscribed in its protagonist to construct a marginal character. As in Hardy's novel, family traits in Gamboa's novel guide the reader through a dialogue with the sciences. Santa's inherited traits are difficult to see because the narrative excessively focuses on patterns of progressive deterioration. Earlier, the story mentions her family, her mother, and her two brothers, with the noticeable absence of the father. In her personal accounts, the narrative presents Santa as a young woman progressing slowly but certainly in all aspects, as the narrator describes "... her existence without clouds, a smooth development, a progressive embellishment ..." (43).[11] This point of departure highlights natural and physical traits without atavism.

However, different from Tess, Santa is depicted with hereditary traits in later commentaries of the narrators. The narrative suggests that Santa brings back her great-great-grandfather's viciousness and lasciviousness. He explains her sexual activity throughout her hereditary traits, as he states the following:

Is it that true that the men deserve to be loved? While she tried to find the answer that would satisfy her doubt, the male parade persisted ... Her good health also persisting, greatly resisting the dog's existence. Santa became more beautiful ... What she was losing, and in a great rush, unfortunately, was the moral sense and all of its fascinating manifestations; she had not even a trace of it, and for the moment, she became acclimated with her new degrading state [and] it is to be presumed that in her blood she carried germs of a very old lasciviousness of a great-great-grandfather who was resurrecting within her with his vices. (69-70)[12]

While the narrative depicts Santa as vicious or lascivious because of her inheritance, it also portrays the character as a public health hazard. Santa's sexual activity is the reason that leads the reader to see her as a danger to public health. Nonetheless, Gamboa frames the story by contrasting the purity of the country and the corruption of the urban, which ultimately corrupts Santa. The protagonist becomes the evil that needs to be removed because of her decay

---

[11] "... una existencia sin nubes, un desarrollo suave, un embellecimiento progresivo ..." (43).

[12] "¿Acaso los hombres merecen ser amados? Mientras hallaba respuesta que satisficiese su duda, persistía el desfile de masculinos ... persistía su buena salud resistiendo a maravilla esa existencia de perros. Santa embelleció más aún ... Lo que sí perdía, y a grandísima prisa, por desgracia, era el sentido moral en todas sus encantadoras manifestaciones; ni rastro quedaba de él, y por lo pronto se connaturalizó con su nuevo y degradante estado, es de presumir que en la sangre llevara gérmenes de muy vieja y lascivia de algún tatarabuelo que en el resucitaba con vicios y todo" (69-70).

(Castillo 177). The passage above gives the reader specific information while trying to provide a pseudo-scientific explanation for Santa's behavior. The first assertion of the narrative is that Santa becomes more beautiful while she inserts herself into a life of prostitution. From the Lombrosian view, prostitutes show specific physical traits that differentiate them from the criminal woman.[13] Recalling the beautifulness is a direct reference to atavism. In other words, the novel highlights the beautiful woman as a possible deviant. Later, the same narrative refers to eugenics, arguing that Santa loses her moral sense while explaining that loss through her inheritance, as in eugenics in practice. An allusion to the concept of "Particulate Inheritance" to describe the transmission of "… traits of features and character— that is to say continuous features and not isolated points" (Galton, *Natural Inheritance* 9).

Gamboa's narrative brings to the fore the idea of "Latent Characteristics," which he suggests are a likeness of the features or character of a child with those of the child's ancestors (Galton *Natural Inheritance* 11). By recalling biological contamination with "germs" and vices, the story references the concept of atavism--that is, inherited factors that return the individual to a primitive state. The passage above, then, makes the only negative reference to a male ancestor of Santa, over whom every inheritable evil falls. Moreover, the novel describes a secondary character as a positivist who represents the state: "the public servant, a furious positivist who used to have breakfast with Lombroso … [,] examines these interesting specimens [;] he knows how to handle them without getting hurt … while studying the ones who inhabit the incurable progress of degeneration" (227).[14] The commentary about Lombroso by the narrator presents the patriarchal control in which he is actively a participant. This reference also recalls the noticeable absence of the father and any information about him. The narrator purposely omits this information to emphasize Santa's environment, education, control, and social presence. It is noticeable that her brothers inherit neither bad traits nor character, nor are they affected by the father's absence. By taking control of the story, the narrator does not let Santa's character react to her misfortune. Additionally, the narrator suggests that the agente del ministerio público (a public servant) is a brilliant and educated man but depicts him only as an observer who points out the inefficiency of the state.

---

[13] Lombroso comments about the prostitutes that they "are almost quite free from wrinkles … and asymmetrical faces: what they have more frequently are … hairiness … and above all anomalous teeth … [T]hey show fewer of the anomalies which produce ugliness, but are marked by more signs of degeneration" (85).

[14] "el agente del ministerio público un positivista furibundo- un científico que se desayunaba con Lombroso … examina sabandijas interesantes, sabe de que ante cogerlas sin que muerdan … estudiando las que habitan los progresos incurables de la degeneración" (227).

In other words, there is no application of the agent's knowledge; rather, he is the representation of the state's failure.

In contrast, Hardy's novel presents a different picture of the woman in the event of Tess killing Alec, a picture in which she frees herself, though she later arrives at deadly consequences. So, Tess brings to the fore a sensation of freedom. Also, it is worth mentioning that the intervention of the state in the character of Tess is effective and strong. Another commentary about control of the environment in the novel *Santa* has to do with the father figure, who is not present, but usually, this figure controls the social interactions, economy, and behaviors. A good example of the father figure can be found in Barragán de Toscano's novel *La hija*, in which Vicente Colombo, the father of the main character, María, is an omnipresent authority in every space of the novel. The lack of a father, then, for the character of Santa, leads the character to her downfall. Santa loses her pregnancy, and later, she falls sick with a severe form of cancer. Biology intervenes in the form of inherited traits. Also, the cancer and the blindness appear in connection with sexual behavior and prostitution. Federico Gamboa dehumanizes the character of Santa using tropes of modernity, such as the mechanized rhythms of the brothel's neighborhood (Castillo 183). The narrator of Gamboa's novel no doubt involves himself in the theme and acts as a discursive voice while engaging in a moral speech designed to guide the reader's perspective. This intervention appears throughout the novel, and its purpose is to influence the reader's moral and political views. Gamboa elicits for the reader the image of a woman with a natural inclination to prostitution in the urban context. This is an issue commented on by José Joaquín Blanco, who suggests that this author is entangled, somehow, in the erotization of "los cuerpos de miseria" (Castillo 177). Such a visual depiction of Gamboa's novel summons the idea of the marginalized individual who becomes an instrument to dominate, like the right hand of the masochist in a mirror reflection (Dijkstra 352). In this sense, the marginal individual helps to illuminate the means of domination and its system of values. Santa, as the marginal lower-class woman in the urban context, positions her in different directions. One direction is to climb the socioeconomic latter and progress in her socioeconomic status. The novel represents this instance when she ends up with the bullfighter El Jarameño, with whom she can have a house and access to upper social strata events. On the other hand, Santa also decays as she moves forward with her life. She separates from El Jarameño and starts to deteriorate rapidly after this.[15] Additionally, women's bodies in cultural production became

---

[15] Bran Dijkstra suggest that in the late nineteenth-century, lower and middle-class women were seen as commodities, but they had access to socioeconomic progress. He also suggests that such as socioeconomic progress was feared by well positioned men.

the focus of interest as an erotic model widely used in Spain, allowing the objectifying vision of consumption of women, as Isabel Clúa indicates. Clúa's assertions, as we see in the context of Gamboa's novel, work very well. Nonetheless, in the novel of Gamboa, the character of Santa not only plays the eroticized woman but also depicts the sick and the living dead woman. In the post-mortem note dedicated to the sculptor Jesus Contreras Santa, located before the first chapter, Santa is allowed to speak: "Don't think that I was a saint [Santa] because that was my name. I was clay and I am clay, my triumphant flesh now in the cemetery ... Embrace me and resurrect me. What does it cost you?" (Gamboa).[16] This depiction of a dead woman speaking brings to the fore the idea that lower and middle-class women's climbing ignited fear in nineteenth-century, well-positioned men. Such an idea resulted in a thematic aesthetic expression depicting women related to death, such as Salome, morphine addicts, syphilitics, and vampires (Dijkstra 360). In addition, the novel uses the power of fear invested in the character of Santa to control the reader's perspective toward women or marginal characters. In this sense, fear becomes a form of power. It constructs the narrator as an agent of social trust while engaging the reader in social mores. Bourdieu's field of cultural production shows the author as a figure that associates with the elite's discourse of power dominance. Federico Gamboa, then, participates as part of the dominant class, an aspect that connects the contexts of the nation-building process and the patriarchal male project. In other words, Gamboa, as part of the *letrado*,[17] the lettered minority, in part, helped to construct the collective idea of the Mexican imaginary. Gamboa, a Mexican diplomat, politician, and writer who worked as an ambassador to the United States and England, expresses sentiments about civilization and barbarism, among others. His expressions on race and vice parallel Galton and Lombroso's thoughts. For example, in his work *Mi Diario* (1920), he suggests that boxing is a barbaric sport:

> It was agreed the combat would last for twenty—*rounds*— just in the tenth [was]a hideous punch. ... When recovering the first man, who shook his hand was the winner ... Oh, Redskins, you are lambs! ... It is a

---

[16] "No vayas a creerme santa, pore así me llamé ... Barro fui y barro soy, mi carne triunfadora se halla en el cementerio ... Acógeme tú y resucítame ¿Qué te cuesta...?" (Gamboa).

[17] The idea of the *letrado* comes historically from the Latin American Criollos who had access to education and so were in charge of politics, education and so forth, a form of continuation of colonial rule. This cultural practice continued during the nineteen century throughout the region. The *letrado* used to come from many fields, but doctors in medicine were many times involved in literary works as writers, Federico Gamboa, in this case, can be highlighted.

shame! That applause, human fights ... Resolutely, the US, in the highest
meaning of the word, is not a totally civilized country. (306)[18]

In this intimate text, Gamboa lets the reader see his inner thoughts in relation
to what he considers barbaric, which he immediately associates with the Native
American population, followed by the comment about the uncivilized United
States. Nonetheless, his narrative in the novel is the instrument with which he
delivers a discourse from the Radical Naturalism perspective. In particular, he
creates a dialogue between the inherited traits of eugenics and alcohol from a
scientific perspective as a form of educative media. Alcohol, in particular, was
one of the main concerns for writers and states around the world at the *fin de
siècle* time. The view of alcohol as a trigger of physical and psychological
anomalies was common among governments and societies (Lilienfeld 3). These
concerns were not the exception in Mexico and in Great Britain, as is clear in
the works of Gamboa and Hardy.

Alcoholism

Tess of the D'Urbervilles differs from the Radical Naturalism approach to the
topics of alcohol and social decadence. Naturalism in England was not
particularly welcomed. For example, British writers such as George Meredith
and George Moore distanced themselves from Zola's Naturalism, arguing that
his scheme pushed human characters toward animalization (Plotz 32-33).
Hardy's narrative is well-balanced; it does not exacerbate the possibilities of its
characters, settings, and so forth. In the recreation of Wessex, Hardy intended
to display his understanding of humanity. He expresses this intent in an
introductory work, "General Preface to the Novels and Poems." Hardy was
particularly interested in psychology, medicine, diagnosis, and other therapeutic
approaches of his time (Fincham 2). The novel still uses aspects of Naturalism
and frames women and men, as well as marginal and non-marginal societies,
to engage the reader in the New Woman perspective. As mentioned above,
Hardy, though a New Woman writer, does not align with eugenics like Sarah
Grand. In this context, the narrative addresses alcohol with negativity,
expressing worries about social decay in rural settings as it presents some cases
of social or biological deterioration.

Very early, the novel shows not only how alcohol is present but also how it
contributes to social decay and economic stagnation in Tess's family. The social

---

[18] "Pactado el combate por veinte as altos—*rounds,*— al décimo la espantosa puñada ... Al
recuperarse el primer hombre que le estrechó la mano fue su vencedor ... ¡Oh, Pieles Rojas,
¡sois corderos! ... ¡qué vergüenza! que aplaude, luchas humanas... Resueltamente, los
EEUU., en la alta acepción de la palabra, no son un país civilizado del todo" (306).

problem in the Wessex countryside is described through depictions of alcohol, as in the instance in which the narrator presents the character of John Durbeyfield, Tess's father:

> On an evening in the latter May a middle-aged man was walking homeward from Shaston to the village of Marlott ... The pair of legs that carried him were rickety, and there was a bias in his gait which inclined him somewhat to the left of a straight line. He occasionally gave a smart nod, as if in confirmation of some opinion, though he was not thinking of anything in particular. An empty egg-basket was slung upon his arm, the nap of his hat was ruffled, a patch being quite worn away at its brim where his thumb came in taking it off. (3)

In the excerpt above, the reader can see how the visual elements that Hardy uses are related to alcohol drinking, as we see John Durbeyfield's way of behaving and walking. The "empty egg-basket" in the evening time raises questions. Is he not bringing eggs for breakfast? Or did he sell all the eggs? And if so, where is the money? In any case, the basket appears as a symbol of economic stagnation. This point also provides information about how Victorians were affected by male dominance since the man was the provider in economic terms. Moreover, setting the tone in this way, the novel prepares the reader to understand later situations. For example, later, the novel confirms that John Durbeyfield has a serious drinking problem that leads to economic devastation, framed in a naturalistic perspective with harsh economic conditions of rural life. As Sara Beliveau explains, Hardy partially uses the structures of Naturalism.

Because of the economy, Tess's father and mother wish to send her to the D'Urberville's house and to marry Alec. In other words, Tess is prostituted by her parents as one of the effects of alcohol (Fincham 243). In contrast with her mother or her father, Tess does not engage in any alcohol drinking, and she does not follow other women in the same behavior.

The women in Hardy's rural society are affected by the same evil of alcohol and by the abuses of the aristocracy or high social class, as the narrator points out:

> Every village has its idiosyncrasy, its constitution, often its own code of morality. The levity of some of the younger women in and about Trantridge was marked, and was perhaps symptomatic of the choice spirit who ruled The Slopes in that vicinity. The place had also a more abiding defect; it drank hard. (75)

Alcohol is present in all cultural and social practices as a routine in Trantridge's daily life in which women actively participate. In addition, such cultural idiosyncrasies imply the concept of continuity; they become customs, as the narrator suggests, "The chief pleasure of these philosophers lay in going every Saturday night ... to Chaseborough, a decayed market-town..." (75). This is a social problem connected with prostitution-like behavior between Trantridge's women/girls and the aristocracy.

Later, in a scene at Chaseborough, alcohol appears in a gathering of rural girls and aristocratic men, one of whom remarks, "'The maids don't think it respectable to dance at "The Flower-de-Luce," ... Besides, the house sometimes shuts up just when their jints begin to get greased. So, we come here and send out for liquor" (78). This depiction unveils how the aristocracy poisons other social strata. Alcohol drinking implicates violence, social decadence, and gender inequality. The excerpt remarks how the aristocracy tangentially promotes these practices. From the premise of criminal anthropology, alcohol sparks violence not only in men but also in women. Alcohol consumption is a characteristic that relates to social Darwinism since an excess of alcohol drinking will lead to social expulsion regardless of profession or social strata (Lombroso 80). Although in the novel, other women participate actively in dancing, drinking, and engaging in sexual encounters with aristocratic males, Tess does not follow this pattern. By comparing Tess with other female characters who use alcohol and behave in a prostitution-like manner, the novel shows how Tess distances herself from these practices.

The narrator does not involve himself as an authority on social atavism. His tone is soft and neutral when he observes the aforementioned Saturday night: "Then these children of the open air, whom even excess of alcohol could scarcely injure permanently, betook themselves to the field-path; and as they went there moved onward with them, around the shadow of each one's head, a circle of opalized light, formed by the moon's rays ..." (84). Nonetheless, the portrayals of alcohol use seem to be a warning about it by presenting it as the main problem in Great Britain's rural life. Social and gender differences seem to be a constant in the novel, though they can be combined with alcohol. Tess's role contributes to the understanding and comparison of the different levels of social and psychological decay of the rural population and aristocracy. Although the novel uses other women to show alcohol as a determinant of health, it delivers the same strong message about men. It happens when the doctor in Shaston suggests to John Durbeyfield that his heart condition has been caused by beer (Fincham 56). This discussion depicts sickness and death as possible outcomes of alcohol, as the doctor suggests that beer is the cause of his growing heart (Fincham 56). Victorian society did not pay too much attention to the working class and its relationship with alcohol; rather, they just assumed that the two were intrinsically connected. This can be explained by the active social Darwinism principles. Then, lower classes tended to be inclined toward these behaviors because they were less civilized, a social Darwinist perspective in action. However, Hardy's narratives critique drinkers in a way that is mostly educative rather than morally charged (Lilienfeld 15). As mentioned above, part of the New Woman endeavor was, for many writers, to educate instead of delivering discursive moral opinions.

The narrator of this novel certainly differs from Gamboa's narrator. The former does not engage in moral ironies or use pejorative language to depict characters or highlight behaviors. Instead, he provides a neutral observation that leads the reader to evaluate each situation. Nonetheless, the depictions in Hardy's novel, particularly in the scenes that include alcohol, alert the reader to its danger. Lilienfeld notices that Hardy uses nuances of the Temperance movement and shows how it was connected with early feminism in the United States.[19] In addition, the Transatlantic analysis of American and British literature revised itself constantly. However, in the scope of this chapter, the commentary of Lilienfeld is relevant because it connects to the modern views of alcoholism in North America that certainly resonated in Mexico by the late nineteenth century and the early twentieth century. During the *porfiriato*, Mexico City's administration struggled with policies to control alcohol, though they did not intend to totally restrain alcohol sales or drinking (Piccato 126-127). Both novels depict the historical context regarding cultural aspects of British and Mexican society and how marginalities interact with other societal strata, as Leitch and Lewis suggest from the cultural studies approach.

Gamboa depicts inherited traits, along with social and physiological concerns in his novel. The narrative constantly expresses social apprehension toward to alcohol and its effects on male and female characters. Gamboa's novel pays special attention to retrogressions caused by alcohol, and the narrative many times focuses on Santa and other secondary characters. Santa exposes herself to alcohol in a series of stages that show the reader how her character progressively deteriorates. For example, on the first night at the brothel, she is exposed to alcohol: "The champagne purred, and the mood became enthusiastically festive beyond any measurement; all of that degenerated into a vulgar orgy, with rude gestures and foul words, unreasonable

---

[19] The "Temperance" movement appeared in the United States at the beginning of the nineteenth century. Its main purpose was to control consuming alcohol because of its harmful effects. The movement was politically active and lasted more than one hundred years with great influences on legislation regarding alcohol in the United States (Tan, Tan, and Zhang 162).

laughter and bestial proposals" (35).[20] The excerpt suggests that the obscene language and gestures are due to the use of alcohol. These characters transform as their behavior degenerates, while the narrator describes this scene with the moral voice of a well-educated man. He uses lexical items such as "bomba alcohólica" ["alcoholic bomb"], for example, to set the tone in regard to the issue, and they highlight Santa's decline:

> ... On two or three occasions, the alcoholic bomb exploded ...[,] it starting with the throwing of two tables and her losing her temper and becoming out of control, throwing glasses and slamming them against the wall ...[,] [a]nd [her] hurling insults with words so out of place that they slammed against the others' cheeks ... [,] and against the dignity of those at whom she directed them. (100)[21]

The effects of alcohol on Santa advance as the narrator explains how she falls and crashes. Furthermore, the story connects drinking alcohol with sex, tragedy, duels, and madness:

> The human mass was stirred by the rhythm of the music; the mouths came together, the hands looked for something and something they found ... [,] an unhealthy delight invaded men and women; they started to show the initial manifestations of the madness that the alcohol causes; the horrible duels, of a lightning duration, of the dying love, which is easy to see in their tragic faces. (199)[22]

Madness and tragedy appear incorporated in a series of stages, actions, and violence. The scene allows the narrator to compare Santa's social and physical falling with the pastoral view of her as a country flower and the town of Chilamistac as a metaphor representing the nation (Ordiz 14). Gamboa puts rural life on display to make social or political comparisons and to better

---

[20] "Corría el *champagne* y los ánimos entusiasmábanse fuera de medida; aquello degeneraba en orgía vulgar, con palabras y ademanes soeces risas destempladas, propuestas bestiales" (35).

[21] "...Y en dos o tres oportunidades estalló la bomba alcohólica ... [,] con su derribo de mesas y sus enarboladas por alto y sus copas volantes estrellándose contra las paredes ... y con sus insultos desentonados, tan soeces que, se diría, también se estrellan contra las mejillas ... [,] y contra la dignidad del quien van disparados" (100).

[22] "La apretada masa humana se agita al compás de la música; las bocas se juntan, las manos buscan algo y algo encuentran...un malsano regocijo se apodera de ellos y ellas; míranse las manifestaciones iniciales de locura que el alcohol genera; los duelos espantosos, de duración de relámpago, de los amores que agonizan, se acusan en las caras trágicas" (199).

highlight aspects of physical, social, and health decay in the characters. While in the countryside, Santa can enjoy her house and animals, in the city, she cannot enjoy her life because of her involvement in prostitution and alcohol. The narrator's perspective lets us see him as a participant in the brothel practices, a position that enhances social failure. Deborah Toner evaluates the relationship between alcohol and madness in the novel and connects Gamboa's critique of modernity and how he underlines alcohol poisoning and the lack of morals among poor rural girls. She also adds that alcohol and madness in *Santa* are representations of the extensive intrusion of politics in literary works. In this sense, Toner reiterates the idea of the *letrado* as an instructive social and political instrument for patriarchal authority. This view also relates to the concept of Bourdieu's field of power, in which the author becomes part of the economic elite and participates in the exercise of power.

Violence is a symptom of alcoholism that is, in part, underlined in the description of the social decay and other regressions in Gamboa's novel. Nonetheless, the story brings to light how alcohol leads to crime:

> The alcohol continued doing its quiet, relentless, and destructive work ...
> The invader [alcohol]opened the prison to swell the ranks, and the armed prisoners left the prisons where custom found them. They go out from their detention that guards the wounded and battered ... [,] the perverse instincts go free, the yeast of crime, the legacy of their delinquent ancestors; they all go out free of chains. [The conscience] informs half of ourselves and the beasts that equal us, the galley that we keep hardened in the jail of the conscience ... The enemy has won. The brain becomes tender ... [;] the discernment is absent. And the results are the savages, primitives, similar to all invading forces, which rape, and kills. (209-211)[23]

The text advances the idea of individuals becoming bestial, which at the time was considered a real possibility by science. At the time, this idea was true for positivists and affected the view of society, creating the perspective of social Darwinism. Then, the novel follows the pattern of the nineteenth-century medical view of alcoholics. At the *fin de siècle*, alcohol is an agent that triggers

---

[23] "El alcohol, en tanto continuaba su obra callada, implacable destructora ... El invasor abrió las cárceles para engrosar las filas, y los presidiarios armados, salen de los presidios que la voluntad custodia herida y maltrecha ... [,] salen los instintos perversos, las levaduras de crimen, los legados de nuestros antepasados delincuentes; salen todos los encadenados, lo que informa la mitad de nuestro ser y a las bestias nos equipara, los galeotes que guardamos aherrojados en los calabozos de la conciencia ... El enemigo a triunfado. El cerebro se entenebrece...el discernimiento se ausenta. Y los resultados son salvajes, primitivos, idénticos a los de todas las invasiones, se estupra, se asesina, de degrada" (209-211).

physical degradation and brings a person to the beast stage. In the excerpt above, the narrator delivers a discourse highlighting the psychological impact of alcohol on these characters. Following the text in the excerpt above, the first word that one notices is "alcohol," then a series of words connected to the biological and psychological evolution/regression. These words are stated as "savage," "primitives," "prison," "prisoner," "detention," and so forth. Gamboa also uses the medical perspective when he refers specifically to atavistic retrogression and the names of body parts, particularly the "brain." Also, the narrator uses the impersonal *se* to direct his ideas. The use of this syntax in Spanish functions to direct the message to a collective audience or undetermined subject. In this sense, the story remarks upon the idea of barbarism and civilization while pointing out that society is going backward because of the abuse of alcohol.

The novel depicts concerns about alcohol and women, and the text clearly shows parallels with Lombroso's points about marginal issues. One of the major topics that disturbs Lombroso more than alcohol is prostitutes, which he analyzes in his book *The Female Offender* (1995). His study separates prostitutes from criminal women, but overall, he concludes that women are more subject to atavism than men: "The remarkable rarity of anomalies … is not a new phenomenon in the female, nor is it in contradiction to the undoubted fact that atavistically she is in nearer to her origin that the male …" (107). Lombroso cannot determine which are the specific characteristics or degenerative characteristics of the criminal woman, but he argues that prostitutes would show more visual degenerative characteristics. One should notice that the material that he uses, the skulls, comes from prostitutes only. This also recalls the proposition of W.K. Brooks when he suggests that females are biologically inferior to males.

The concept of bio-power is also recurrent in this novel, along with normativity and regulatory measurements. The regulations were not made to be understood by anyone but to be clarified through a series of measurements and statistical data presented as a valid outcome of a study that empowered and legitimized the control of the body. In the novel, the prominent figure of the doctor in medicine, science, and ultimately politics, emerged as a tool to control population and ideologies. This concept can be extended to Mexico, Spain, England, or the United States, in which the medical discourse is present too. For example, in Spain, the author of *La prostituta* (1884), Eduardo López Bago, was a doctor in medicine. Here, with the comparative approach, one sees the counterargument between the Radical Naturalism of Gamboa and the New Woman perspective of Thomas Hardy, revealing how bio-power worked in late nineteenth-century society.

Additionally, while addressing the themes of inhered traits, alcohol, social degeneration, and atavism inscribed in the female characters, both novels underline and converge in depictions of some cultural expressions while entangling gender discourses. *Santa* and *Tess* raise concerns about the situation of women and how they become vulnerable to the victimization of prostitution, especially through alcohol. They diverge, nonetheless, in the way the plots of both novels develop these approaches while including discussions about other cultural and social practices.

Tess displays a social fabric structured in a feudal-like stratification in which women can be understood as the bottom of a hierarchy. Tess is the epitome of honesty, charity, tenderness, courageousness, resiliency, and overall, all the good traits that a woman may have. This comes with the caveat that no man in the novel shows such strength. In addition, she is an ambiguous character. She is a self-sufficient and hard-working woman, and she does not engage in alcohol drinking or purposely engage in prostitution or prostitution-like behaviors. She differs from the other female characters in the novel, who display a different social behavior embedded in patriarchal dominance. The focus of the narrative allows the reader to see this community and its cultural practices in which the gender discourse is vibrantly present.

Drunkenness is a specific characteristic in the town of Trantridge in which men and women are entangled with alcohol. This situation presents the discreet participation of the young women of the community in prostitution-like behavior: "The maids don't think it respectable to dance at "The Flower-de-Luce," ... 'They don't like to let everybody see which be their fancy-men" (78). As Alec d'Urberville suggests, the fancy-men are aristocrats who provide the alcohol to the young women. On the other hand, the economic stagnation of the region is clearly present in Tess's house in combination with heavy alcohol use. Tess's mother suggests to her that she should dress more attractively and to pretend to go to work:

> Her mother expostulated. 'You will never set out to see your folks without dressing up more the dand and that?'
> 'But I am going to work!' said Tess.
> 'Well, yes, said Mrs. Durbeyfield; and in a private tone, 'at first there mid be a little pretence o't ... But I think it will be wiser of 'ee to put your best side outward,' she added. 'Very well; I suppose you know best,' replied Tess with calm abandonment. (56; ellipsis in original)

The interest of Tess's mother and father is more related to economics and alcohol, as Fincham suggests. This fragment reflects a common cultural practice in which the middle- or lower-class girls are pushed to entangle with the aristocracy. The practice in rural settings antagonizes Victorian social views. When one looks carefully at the depictions of these cultural practices, the text not only raises questions about the patriarchal dominance over women but also questions the future of young women and rural society in Great Britain. In addition, the narrative inquiries about the women in this context, which differs from the urban scenery. It gives a different perspective on the opportunities of women in Victorian society.

Moreover, this domain is extended to older women who police and manage young women's sexuality (Mayer 8), as we see in the scene of Tess coming back home and her mother wanting her to marry Alec:

> "Have you come home to be married?'
> 'No, I have not come for that mother.' …
> Why didn't ye think of doing some good for your family instead o' thinking only of yourself? See how I've got to teave and slave and your poor weak father with his heart clogged like a dripping-pan." (103)

All the inquiries come from the mother in the name of the father, a scenario reflecting male dominance in the control of sons and daughters through the mother. In other words, the novel puts in front of the reader not only a tragedy of a rural community in the context of nineteenth-century Great Britain but also the tragedy of the young women. In this segment also, the reader learns the involvement of Tess's parents in her marital status, hoping she marries Alec.

Framed in Radical Naturalism, the novel *Santa* does not deviate from tragedy and raises questions about gender in cultural, sociological, and medical interpretations of atavism. The story reflects worries about the young girls' rural life as they appear in the main character's *historia* in the second chapter. The idea of modernity that appears in the countryside of Mexico is reflected in this chapter in the form of the alférez Marcelino Beltrán (Ordiz 12). This character, a military ensign and representative of the state, entangles Santa in a relationship, leaving her dishonored. This is an important cultural aspect of the novel in that it is male dominance in combination with state power that allows the character of Santa to be expelled from her house. The expulsion from her house not only depicts how the family deals with dishonor but also prepares Santa for the brothel. In the expulsion of the impure woman, there is a cultural component that shows Catholic values.

Other cultural practices surface with the use of liquor in different forms, mostly in the brothel space. The most notorious is the progressive deterioration of Santa, in which she falls not only socially but also biologically as she uses alcohol throughout the novel. Many depictions show different aspects of the protagonist that are intended to represent determinism. This, for example, appears in a scene with the Jalameño: "Wounded in her vanity because of the ill-concealed diversion of the bullfighter, who did not pay attention to her, [she], and propelled by such antipathy, did her best to lavish attention on some other gentlemen who competed with one another in praises and pampering for her; she sat on top of this one, or drank from the other one's cup" (79).[24] In each gathering in this context, liquor is present, and Santa uses it, each time degrading herself. The voice of the narrator allows the reader to understand the type of gathering that happens when Santa appears. The narrative line lets one see an entertainer, a bullfighter, and a historical Spanish cultural icon significant across all social strata. The bullfighter represents a nostalgic connection between colonial Spain and the recently born Mexican nation. These cultural icons that crossed the Atlantic Basin were factors of unification between Spain and Latin America. Second, the *señoritos* in the story represented the young men of high society. In other words, the narrator describes the role of alcohol in the cross-section of Mexican men who gather in the social margins. In addition, this narrator unveils the patriarchal perspective of men over women while he states with certainty Santa's sentiments and emotions in a neutral medical voice. In both depictions, the cultural component raises questions about the social uses of alcohol while, at the same time, it uses Santa as a model of decadence in biological and social hierarchies. The Mexican high social class at the *fin de siècle* time was mostly interested in the modernization of the city while arousing social anxiety about criminality in specific zones (Piccatto 114-115). Both novels converge in centering concerns about rural young women and their exposure to liquor, prostitution, and other cultural practices in Mexico and Great Britain. The narratives diverge in their regard to gender discourse, through which Santa's perspective uses the decay model to create a view of social Darwinism, atavism, crime, and human decadence. In contrast, though a model of a victim, Hardy's novel depicts the aristocracy's patriarchal perspective and dominance and how alcohol influences the story's world toward social decadence.

Conclusion

To conclude, the concepts of atavism, eugenics, and liquor consumption consequences in Hardy's novel demonstrate opposition to the scientific perspectives of Lombroso and Galton, while Gamboa's novel uses those concepts to criticize the state's affairs. Nonetheless, Hardy presents these scientific perspectives to construct the character of Tess as a strong woman

---

[24] "Herida en su vanidad por el mal disimulado desvío del torero, que no volvió a parar mientes en ella; impulsada por la antipatía, esmeróse en prodigar a los señoritos que se la disputaban halagos y mimos; se sentó encima de éste bebió en la compa de aquél ..." (79).

who differs greatly from the male character. Hardy's novel imprints Tess with tenacity, resiliency, and other virtues that she has not directly received from her parents. Similarly, these comparisons allow us to see the reflection of class dynamics in rural settings embedded in the portrayal of cultural practices. These traits help to underline different virtues and the vulnerability of the character of Tess. Biologically inherited traits and atavisms are shown in many instances, but throughout the scene of Sorrow, the reader can infer a link between the weakness of Tess's father and that of Alec d'Urberville. In addition, this theme also raises questions regarding biological weakness, the social structure, the abusive attitude of the aristocracy, and the place of patriarchal dominance of the novel's social landscape. All these practices of social Darwinism are clearly depicted in the abusive behavior of the aristocracy or the rich families, but they are particularly present in the relationship between Alec and Tess. Overall, this aspect of the novel highlights the role of rural women and their important value in daily life. This fiction elevates the valuable presence of rural women, whose health and heritage historiography was erased in England at the time.

Hardy's novel portrays the issue of drinking alcohol in all of Wessex but around Trantridge. Liquor penetrates the entire social fabric of the novel. It represents the main source of Tess's problems at home and outside of it. Her parents' heavy drinking triggers a series of manipulations that help Alec's sexual attack on Tess, which is the beginning of her misfortunes. Alcohol is also used in underground settings in prostitution-like gatherings between aristocratic young men and rural low/middle-class young women. Both situations revise the social construction of Trantridge. These questions show how this community uses liquor and how it pulls rural society backward. The narrative line throughout illustrates the comparisons between Tess and other characters and how Victorian cultural practices, costumes, and values are inoperative. This dynamic is emphasized in the victimization of the main character in a multiplicity of ways. The novel, nonetheless, parallels Lombroso's worries about alcohol, which seem to be a worldwide trend.

Gamboa's novel similarly addresses these themes with a narrator who regards himself as an authority on Santa, women, and health. The story becomes a hyperbolic expression that emphasizes moral judgments and medical terms referring to the character of Santa. In this discourse, the idea of eugenics is possible through comparisons between Santa and secondary characters who act as concomitants. The absence of the father is notorious, but his figure is linked with an ancestor with bad genes, suggesting that at least one male ancestor has affected Santa in the present, a parallel with Galton's eugenics. Gamboa's and Hardy's narratives share the same social Darwinism representations, particularly regarding alcohol and social class interactions.

Also, like Hardy's, Gamboa's work addresses the worries about alcohol through and through. The narrative arranges and frames the main character in a progressive model of a liquor drinker who degenerates physically and psychologically. Throughout these aspects, the novel presents the social decadence in which high social classes, politicians, or public servants are not only in decline through liquor but also serve as evidence of the practice of social Darwinism. Cultural traits are embedded in the narrative while all parts of the society represented by men march through the brothel. This depiction positions the brothel as a gathering place for men, who display their dominance over marginal places and subjects. The novel delivers its gender discourse from the perspective of male domination in which women are the focus and the target of atavism, crime, and social and human degeneration. Both novels represent respective cultural practices in which women are the focus. While Santa is the representation of deviancies, regressions, and atavism, Tess is a tragedy and the epitome of the failure of Victorian values and virtues. These novels explore rural and urban landscapes in which social Darwinism operates and underlines crossed social boundaries as a trend in cultural practices. This convergence becomes significant since the two cultures are separated by the Atlantic Basin, by cultural perspectives, racial beliefs, and, most of all, by language.

Conclusion

The unique comparisons of literary works and geographical dimensions of this work reveal how the New Woman perspective creatively constructs female characters differently from Radical Naturalism. These constructions, many times, use the model of Radical Naturalism to give rise to a gendered dialogue in which the texts give women's representations a more real and possible path to success. Pardo Bazán's *La gota de sangre* presents Chulita Ferna, a fallen woman who is a victim and Selva, the narrator, who allows her to avoid punishment for her involvement in the crime. Also, Petronila in "Tío Terrones" succeeds economically after being expelled from her house. Similarly, Tess is a victim of patriarchal power, her family, aristocracy, and society, but she is resilient, healthy, and brave. Her strong physical and psychological traits make it evident that Hardy deviates from classic Naturalism. Another female character who stands out is Ideala of Grand's narrative. Her text offers a New Woman environment in which Ideala is a victim of her husband. She confronts the patriarchal pillars of society and later succeeds in all aspects of her life. Grand's works, similar to Pardo Bazán's, present a female character who criticizes women's condition in the *fine de siècle* era. Hence, this work lets us see how different spaces and liminalities are present in the works of Gamboa, Hardy, Pardo Bazán, and Chopin. The protagonist of Gamboa's text, Santa, is enclosed, most of the time, in the brothel in which crime and deviancies are evident. The New Woman perspective in texts by Hardy or Pardo Bazán gives the reader a broader possible space in which crime is present. In *Tess,* the inns and the countryside are places that allow crime to happen. For example, Alec's sexual attack on Tess shows how Hardy creatively frames his main character, Tess, as a victim in the rural landscape. Pardo Bazán in *La gota de sangre* uses the house in an aristocratic old neighborhood as a space to frame prostitution. By comparing Pardo Bazán and Gamboa's works, I hope to demonstrate an intentional gendered dialogue present in both narratives and issues related to their authorship sex. As Joyce Tolliber points out, Leopoldo Alas Clarín constantly and harshly criticized the female characters of Pardo Bazán's works. He argued that her works were not naturalist. Clarín's comments feature a conversation based on gender that is reflected in Pardo Bazán's representations of women. In contrast to Pardo Bazán's experience as a female author, Gamboa's work *Santa* was a "success" in Mexico and in Latin America. Authorship's sex was a significant factor that influenced women's writings during the late nineteenth and early twentieth century. Moreover, in England, the New Woman female authors were criticized harshly, mostly by male critics.

In Chapter 3, I find cultural similarities between Hardy and Gamboa. The comparison between *Tess* and *Santa* brings to the forefront depictions of social Darwinism regarding women as victims, while clearly, both authors raise questions about social class and the role of women in society. They depict social Darwinism as a cultural practice across the social spectrum, and they display similarities in their cultures from both sides of the Atlantic Basin. So, the Transatlantic perspective allows us to see how the late nineteenth century created harsh practices that affected women. More research in this vein might be needed to find specific patterns of social behavior reflected in literature. Most of all, what stands out over all the novels is that the female character is never a New Woman. The New Woman novels depict female characters as submissive women who become agents of change, while in the naturalistic perspective, the female character embodies the patriarchal desire for a woman. As mentioned before, these works also participated in the dialogue between gender perspectives, but they expanded it through the social and scientific sciences. Overall, the Transatlantic perspective gains relevance over other theoretical frameworks discussed here because it lets us compare and realize patterns of conceptualizations about gender and women across the Atlantic Ocean.

Nonetheless, I address the female characters in literary works in the nineteenth-century context from the gendered and the Transatlantic perspectives, addressing themes such as the *femme fatale*, heterotopic spaces, atavism, liminality, visions from eugenics and criminal anthropology in works from Spain, Mexico, the United States and Great Britain. Hardy's and Gamboa's novels seem to culturally converge in the view of women as the representation of the nation or the nation's values. One of the values is the racial purity of the country woman, who is depicted in both novels as an alternative resource for the nation's racial purification. Nonetheless, both novels deconstruct this view by highlighting the political and social perspectives through the social practices they depict. In Hardy's novel, Tess is described as "A Pure Woman," who is victimized by her family, by society, and by the aristocracy. Santa's path is not different. She falls because of a lack of authority. She becomes a victim of the state, represented by Marcelino, and she is expelled from the house by her family. The countryside women and their contamination are clearly an important concern for both novels. In these novels, the women's representations are also linked with alcohol, inherited traits, atavism, and social Darwinism as part of the social and cultural reflection of these works. In *Santa*, the main character's alcoholism shows her progressive deterioration as the novel's accounts move forward. The character of Santa suffers all the effects caused by alcohol; the one most highlighted by the narrative is madness. Male characters and the use of alcohol are also part of the depiction of crime and atavism. Social Darwinism is expressed many times, but the narrator uses Santa as an example of the impossibility of moving upward socially, economically, physically, and psychologically. In Hardy's novel, alcohol takes devastating tolls on health and society, as it plays an important role in the relationship between aristocratic men and countryside girls and women. It is also an element that is used by aristocratic men to poison female characters of the countryside. Lastly, eugenics and atavism are present in this novel as they appear in the form of hereditary traits related to health. Here, the novel evokes and contradicts the idea of the countryside women as a last resort for the Anglo-Saxon race as they are poisoned not only with alcohol but also with STDs. Each novel addresses these problematic issues differently. While Gamboa's narrator tries to convince the reader of the dangers of degeneration, sickness, and lack of mores throughout the character of Santa in the brothel, Hardy's narrative contradicts the eugenics premises. On the contrary, Tess, as a victim, is the epitome of the failure of Victorian values in the countryside.

In addition, Hardy, Gamboa, Pardo Bazán, Barragán de Toscano, and Chopin employ the theme of the spaces such as the brothel, the cave, the countryside, the inns, the house, and the beach as heterotopias that act as elements to frame female characters under social death, liminality, deviancies, and/or crime. These spaces highlight social and gender implications in marginal zones interacting with liminal subjects. The novels offer multiple scenarios in which nonnormative sexuality and sexual behaviors are allowed. It is important to highlight that liminality foregrounds "social death" and "the rite of passage," which appear in all the novels.

These events not only allow the characters to change their identity but also permit them to move across social boundaries. María and Tess change their last name and become part of the society, while Julia Fernandina becomes Chulita Ferna. Lastly, the case of Santa differs from the others because it is decided that her name will arouse eroticism in the brothel's clientele. The house, the brothel, the inns, the cave, the countryside, and the beach are depictions of heterotopias permitting the characters nonnormative activities while creating liminal subjects. The house's composition in Gamboa's novel is worth mentioning because it can be a potential heterotopia in which the mother, the old woman of the house, controls the sexuality of all the siblings. In this scenario of the house, Santa becomes the representation of the nation in times of nation-building; thus, she needs to be protected.

The *femme fatale* and the woman destined to fall still resonates in literary works around the world. In this work, however, the theme of the marginalized women operates in Radical Naturalism as a patriarchal scheme in which the female character is slowly diluted from sickness to death caused by her sexual behavior. For example, in *Santa*, the main character is primarily depicted as an innocent girl from the countryside of Mexico whose fault is falling in love with a military man. Dishonored and with no other choice but to turn to prostitution and alcohol, she slowly dies. Gamboa follows the pattern well known from Flaubert's *Madame Bovary* (1856), which Emile Zola discusses in his purposeful natural depiction of society in *The Experimental Novel* and practices in *Nana* (1880). All these novels present the same pattern worked by other authors of Radical Naturalism, one in which the woman plays an important role as an irregular element in most cases.

Nonetheless, in *La hija del bandido,* Barragán de Toscano gives the reader a different model of the female character. María, the main character, represents the Mexican woman and her values. She is courageous, and in her role, she resolves the conflict of the novel, destroying the father's authority. In addition, she overcomes the sin of her father toward society by entering a convent, renouncing marriage, and becoming a nun. The character of María prioritizes the practice of Catholicism, one of the main traits of the Mexican woman. This novel significantly deviates from the naturalistic perspective and positions the woman in an opposite place. Overall, María is a highlighted character in the entire story, which takes the center of attention away from the male bandit character. She not only is more effective in restoring the order of the novel but also gains the authority that her father has while giving it to the Catholic view of the woman.

Similarly significant, the novels of Emilia Pardo Bazán and Sarah Grand use the same structure of the *femme fatale,* but they give an alternative ending to the female characters. In *Ideala,* Grand allows the main character to go to China and later work with marginal women. In "Tio Terrones," Pardo Bazán lets the female character not only live, but also become economically successful. Thomas Hardy and Kate Chopin frame their main characters, Tess and Edna, respectively, with a final death. Although in Hardy's and Chopin's narratives, the use of Naturalism is evident, and Tess and Edna finally die, these characters challenge patriarchal dominance. In both novels, the naturalistic structure is broken. Special attention should be paid to the links between Hardy and Gamboa, who diverge and converge with different topics while they use the female character as the main focus of the narrative.

Overall, the comparisons in this work demonstrate the usefulness of Zola's proposals for Naturalism and how patriarchal forces used those proposals in the literature. Here, one sees how the patriarchal power used literary works for the purposes of societal control by articulating deceptive social and biological constructions of the women and, at the same time, how creatively the New Woman authors used the same elements to deconstruct the image of women by presenting different possible outcomes for them. New Woman authors tended to deviate from the idea of determinism in women and put their female characters closer to free will. This creative and resourceful strategy of the New

Woman perspective's uses of literature encourages one to keep looking and researching different examples of the themes discussed above.

One of the limitations, though paradoxical, is the richness of the multiple aspects of the human being, making it impossible to cover them all. So, this research must continue while paying special attention to the New Woman writers addressing the female characters, spaces, social Darwinism, or eugenics. Chronologically, as the focus of the work is the late nineteenth century, comparative research is possible with other works that belong to the nineteenth century and beyond. Authorially, comparisons by the author are rich, no doubt, since all of them have a great deal of literary production. So, analysis can be made from different perspectives of literary criticism, from novels to short stories. One could research the juxtapositions of these literary works with comparative law. Geographically, the Atlantic Basin alone, as a point of departure, invites one to bring to the forefront ideas for future literary exploration. Latin American literature offers a wonderful variety of authors who can be studied through the themes I work on here. Among others from Argentina, for example, we can mention Lucio V. Masila or Emma de la Barra. From Colombia, the writer Jose María Vargas Vila, or from Spain, Eduardo López Bago, Alas Clarín, or Benito Pérez Galdós. In addition, the Anglo-American perspective of the New Woman can also be found in Edith Wharton, another who will enhance my proposals to study.

Thematically, the topics that this book presents can be interpreted in multiple directions. For example, the theme of marginal spaces can be expanded under the perspectives of Henri Lefebvre, Edward Soja, Barthes, and Leigh Mercer, which provides the theoretical background to build arguments about space. This also occurs in other Spanish literatures in which women inhabit marginal spaces, as in some narratives of Benito Pérez Galdós (G. Miller 5). All these aspects, no doubt, will greatly guide the upcoming literary examinations from an interdisciplinary perspective.

Work Cited

Albarrán, Fernando V. "Journeys to the Catacombs: Forbidden People and Spaces in Modern Madrid." *Writing Wrongdoing in Spain 1800-1936: Realities, Representations, Reactions.* Edited by Alison Sinclair and Samuel Llano. Tamesis, 2017, pp. 237-256.

Altamirano, Manuel I. *Clemencia* (1869). Berbera Editores, 2006.

———. *El Zarco, the Blue-Eyed Bandit: Episodes of Mexican life Between 1861-1863.* Edited and translated by Ronald Christ. Lumen Books, 2007.

Alvarado, Ana María. "Función del prostíbulo en *Santa y Juntacadávres.*" *Hispanic Journal,* no. 2, vol. 2, 1980, pp. 57-68.

Arnavon, Cyrille. "An American *Madame Bovary*" *The Awakening.* 1899. Norton Critical Edition, Edited by Margo Culley. Seven Treasures Publications, 2008.

Barragán De Toscano, Refugio. *La hija del bandido o los subterráneos del nevado* 1887. Stockcero, 2007.

Barroso, Fernando J. *El naturalismo en la Pardo Bazán.* Plaza Mayor S. A, 1973.

Beliveau, Sara. "Rethinking English Naturalism: Feminine Decadence Hardy's Tess and the French Context." *Excavatio.* vol. XI, 1998, pp. 108-118.

Benjamin, Walter. "The Task of the Translator." *Transatlantic Literary Studies: A Reader.* Edited by Susan Manning and Andrew Taylor. The Johns Hopkins UP, 2007, pp. 172-181.

Bentley, Nancy. "Women, Realist Authorship." *Cambridge History of American Literature.* Edited by Sacvan Bercovitch. Cambridge UP, 2008, pp. 137-180.

Berra, Tim. "What Darwin Said." Charles Darwin: *The Concise Story of and Extraordinary Man.* John Hopkins UP, 2009, pp. 68-69.

Blanco, José Joaquín. *Cuando todas las chamacas se pusieron medias nylon (y otras crónicas).* Joan Boldó i Climent, 1988.

Bliss, Katherine Elaine. *Compromise Position Prostitution Public Health and Gender Politics in Revolucionary Mexico City.* Pensilvania Satate UP, 2001.

Bolea, Castejón Ramón. "Los médicos de la higiene: Medicina y prostitución en la España contemporánea (1847-1918). *Bulletin d'Hisorie Contemporaine de l'Expgne,* vol. Juin, no. 25, 1997, pp. 73-86.

Borges, Jorge L. "Translators of the One Thousand and One Nights." Translated by Esther Allen. *The Translation Studies Reader.* Edited by Lawrence Venuti. Routledge, 2012, pp. 92-106.

Boumelha, Penny, "The Patriarchal of Class: *Under the Tree, Far from the Madding Crowd, the Woodlanders. The Cambridge Companion to Thomas Hardy.* Edited by Dale Kramer. The U of Cambridge P, 1999, pp. 130-144.

Bourdieu, Pierre. *The Field of Cultural Production.* Columbia UP, 1993.

Brady, Kristine. "Thomas Hardy and matters of gender." *The Cambridge Companion to Thomas Hardy.* Edited by Dale Kramer, Cambridge UP, 1999, pp. 93-111.

Brooks, Keith W. *The Law of* Heredity: *A Study of the Case of Variation, and the Origin of Living Organisms.* John Murphy, 1883.

Brushwood, John S. "La novela mexicana frente al porfirismo." *Historia Mexicana,* vol.7, no. 3, 1958, pp. 368-405.

Bulmer, Michael. "Eugenics." *Francis Galton: Pioneer of Heredity and Biometry.* Johns Hopkins UP, 2003, pp. 79-101.

Butkus, Clarine., M., Christian Fleury, Benoit Raoulx. "Desiring the Shore: Adolphe Lalyre and the Sirens of Carteret." *Shima* vol. 12, no. 2, 2018, pp. 104-125.

Cánovas, Rodrigo. "Lectura gratuita de la novela "Santa" de Federico Gamboa." *Revista Chilena de Literatura,* no, 59,2019, pp. 81-98.

Castillo, Debra A. "Meat Shop Memories: Federico Gamboa's *Santa.*" *INTI* vol. 40, no, 41, 1994, pp. 175-192.

Chopin, Kate. *The Awakening.* 1899. Norton Critical Edition, Edited by Margo Culley. Seven Treasures Publications, 2008.

Christensen, Nelson Caroline. "Introduction." *A New Woman Reader.* Edited by Caroline Christensen Nelson. Broadview P, 2001, pp. vii-xxx.

Clúa, Isabel. "De mercancías y vendedoras: Las paradojas de la celebridad. *Cuerpos de Escándalo: Celebridad femenina en el fin-de-siècle.* Icaria Acadnueva, 2016, pp. 35-62.

Cooppan, Vilashini. "World Literature and Global Theory: Comparative Literature for the New Millennium (2001)." *World Literature: A Reader.* Edited by Theo D'haen, Césas Domínguez, and Rosendahl Thomsen. Routledge, 2013, pp. 176-197.

Damrosch, David. "What is World Literature?" (2003) *World Literature: A Reader.* Edited by Theo D'haen, César Domínguez, and Rosendahl Thomsen. Routledge, 2013, pp. 198-206.

Deleuze, Giles and Felix Guattari. "Introduction: Rhizome." *Transatlantic Literary Studies: A Reader.* Edited by Susan Manning & Andrew Taylor. The Johns Hopkins U P, 2007, pp. 226-231.

Delgado-Fernández, Miguel. "Un cuento satírico en medio del debate sobre el darwinismo en México." *Alambique: Revista Académica de ciencia ficción y fantasía.* vol. 2, no. 1, 2014, pp. 1-8.

Demolins, Edmond. *Anglo-Saxon Superiority: To What it is Due* (1899). R. F. Fenno & Company, 1899.

Derrida, Jaques. "Letter to a Japanese Friend." *Derrida and Différamce.* Edited by David Wood and Robert Bernasconi. Northwestern UP, 1988, pp. 1-6.

D'haen, Theo, César Domínguez, and Rosendahl Thomsen. "Introduction." *World Literature: A Reader.* Edited by Theo D'haen, Césas Domínguez, and Rosendahl Thomsen. Routledge, 2013, pp. x-xiii.

———. "Reading Paths." *World Literature: A Reader.* Edited by Theo D'haen, Césas Domínguez, and Rosendahl Thomsen. Routledge, 2013, pp. xiii-xxi.

Dickens, Charles. *Bleak House.* 1852. Penguin Classics, 2003.

Didi-Huberman, Georges. *The Invention of Hysteria: Charcot and the Photographic Iconography of the Salpêtrière.* Translated by Alisa Hartz. The MIT P, 2004.

Dijkstra, Bram. *Idols of Perversity: Fantasies of Feminine Evil in the Fin-de-Siècle Culture.* Oxford UP, 1986.

Fernández, Ojea María Elena. "Narrativa feminista en los cuentos de la condesa de Pardo Bazán." *EPOS*, vol. XVI, 2000, pp. 157-176.

Fernández, Pura. "Introducción." *La prostituta: Novela médico-social.* 1884. Renacimiento Biblioteca de Rescate, 2005.

Filgueira Ganzo, Jesus. "Observaciones sobre el espacio en *Isolación.*" *Moenia,* vol. 8, 2002, pp. 79-102.

Fincham, Tony. *Hardy the Physician: Medical Aspects of the Wessex Tradition.* Palgrave Macmillan, 2008.

Foucault, Michel. "Bio-Power." *The Foucault Reader.* Edited by Paul Rabinow. Pantheon Books, 1984, pp. 257-289.

———. *Discipline & Punish: The Birth of the Prison.* Vintage Books, 1991.

———. "Of Other Spaces: Utopias and Heterotopias." *Architecture/Mouvement/ Continuité,* October 1984, pp. 1-9.

———. *The Birth of the Clinic.* Routledge, 1973.

———. "The Order of Discourse." *Untying the Text: A Post-Structuralist Reader.* Edited by Robert Young. Routledge, 1981, pp. 64-78.

Frye, Northrop. "Archetypal Criticism." *Anatomy of Criticism: Four Essays.* Princeton UP, 1973, pp. 131-223.

Galton, David J., and Clare J Galton. "Francis Galton: and Eugenics Today." *Journal of Medical Ethics.* vol. 24, no. 2, 1998, pp. 99-105.

Galton, Francis. *Hereditary Genius* (1869). Macmillan and Co, 1869.

———. *Inquiries into Human Faculty and its Development.* Macmillan, 1883.

———. *Natural Inheritance* (1894). Macmillan and Co, 1894.

———. "Possible Improvement of the Human Breed Under Exiting Conditions of Law Sentiment." *Essays in Eugenics* (1909). The Eugenics Education Society, 1909, pp. 1-34.

Gamboa, Federico. *Mi Diario: Primera Serie— III* (1920). Ediciones Botas México, 1920.

———. *Santa.* 1903. Drácena ficciones y relatos, 2013.

García-Guerrero, Isaac. "Exhibición de Atrocidades: Andalucismo y Degeneración Racial Española en *Insolación* de Emilia Pardo Bazán." *Hispanic Review,* Autum, 2017, pp. 441-465.

Garner, Paul. "'El imperio informal' Británico en América Latina: ¿Realidad o ficción?" *Historia Mexicana,* vol. 65, no. 2, 2015, pp.541-559.

Gatrell, Simon. "Wessex." *The Cambridge Companion to Thomas Hardy.* Edited by Dale Kramer, Cambridge UP, 1999, pp. 19-37.

Gennep, Van-Arnol. *The Rites of Passage.* The U of Chicago P. 1960.

Giles, Paul. "Virtual Subjects: Transnational Fictions and the Transatlantic Imaginary." *Virtual Americas: Transnational Fictions and the Transatlantic Imaginary.* Duke UP, 2002, pp. 1-21.

Grand, Sara. Development?" *Sex, Social Purity and Sarah Grand.* Edited by Ann Heilmann and Stephanie Forward. Routledge, 2000, pp. 556-7.

———. *Ideala,* 1888. Valancourt Books, 2008.

———. "Marriage Questions in Fiction." *Sex, Social Purity and Sarah Grand.* Edited by Ann Heilmann and Stephanie Forward. Routledge, 2000, pp. 77-91.

———. Should Married Women Follow Professions?" *Sex, Social Purity and Sarah Grand.* Edited by Ann Heilmann and Stephanie Forward. Routledge, 2000, pp. 257-9.

———. "The New Aspect of the Woman Question:" *Sex, Social Purity and Sarah Grand.* Edited by Ann Heilmann and Stephanie Forward. Routledge, 2000, pp. 29-35.

———. "The Wrong Road" (1895) *The Illustrated Magazine* vol. 14, March, 1895, pp. 221-228.

Guelke, Jeanne Kay, and Karen Morint. "Gender, Nature, Empire: Women Naturalist in the Nineteenth Century British Travel Literature." *Royal Geographical Society.* Wiley-Blackwell, 2001, pp. 306-326.

Guereña, Jean-Luis. "La historia de la prostitución en España siglos XIX y XX." *Bulletin d'Hisorie Contemporaine de l'Expgne,* vol. Juin, no. 25, 1997, pp. 29-36.

Hardy, Thomas. 1891. *Tess of the D'Urbervilles.* Harper and Brothers Publishers, 1891.

———. "General Preface to the Novels and Poems." *Tess of the D'Urbervilles.* Harper and Brothers Publishers, 1891, pp. vii-xx.

———. "The Profitable Reading of Fiction." *Thomas Hardy Personal Writings.* Edited by Harold Orel. Macmillan, 1967, pp.110-124.

Harvey, Geoffrey. *The Complete Critical Guide to Thomas Hardy.* Routledge, 2003.

Heilmann, Ann. "Femininities: Sarah Grand (1854-1943)." *New Woman Strategies: Sarah Grand, Oliver Schreiner, Mona Caird.* Manchester UP, 2004, pp. 13-80.

———. *New Woman Fiction: Women Writing First-Wave Feminism.* MacMillan P Ltd, 2000.

———. *New Woman Strategies: Sarah Grand, Olive Schreiner, Mona Caird.* Manchester UP, 2004.

———. *"The Awakening* and New Woman Fiction." *The Cambridge Companion to Kate Chopin.* Edited by Janet Beer. Cambridge UP, 2008, pp. 73-104.

Heilmann, Ann and Stephanie Forward, Editors. *Sex, Social Purity, and Sarah Grand.* Routledge, 2000.

Heilmann, Ann., and Mark Llewellyn. "On the Neo-Victorian, Now and Then." *A New Companion to Victorian Literature and Culture.* Edited by Herbert F. Tucker, Wiley Blackwell, 2014, pp. 475-491.

Hildebrand, Molly., J. "Masculine Sea: Gender, Art, and Suicide in Kate Chopin's *The Awakening.*" *American Literary Realism,* vol. 48, no. 3, 2016, pp. 189-208.

Hong, Wehnui. "Space and Female Subjectivity in Kate Chopin's *The Awakening.*" *Comparative Literature: East & West.* Vol. 14, no. 1, 2011, pp. 86-96.

Horcasitas-Urías, Beatriz. "El determinismo Biológico del darwinismo social a la sociología criminal." *Revista Mexicana de Sociología,* vol. 58, no. 4, 1996, pp. 99-126.

Howell, Elmo. "Kate Chopin and the Creole Country." *Louisiana History: The Journal of the Louisiana Historical Association,* vol. 20, no. 2, 1979, pp. 209-219.

Ingardern, Roman. *The Literary Work of Art.* Northwest UP, 1973.

Jakobson, Roman. "'On Linguistic Aspects of Translation.'" *Transatlantic Literary Studies: A Reader*. Edited by Susan Manning and Andrew Taylor. The Johns Hopkins UP, 2007, pp. 182 -183.

Joyce, Simon. *Modernism and Naturalism in British and Irish Fiction 1880-1930*. Cambridge UP, 2014.

Klein, S. Herbert. *The Middle Passage: Comparative Studies in the Atlantic Slave Trade*. Princeton UP, 2017.

Lacey, Nicola. *Women, Crime and Character*. Oxford UP, 2008.

LaGreca, Nancy. "Coming of Age (NCY)." *Rewriting Womanhood: Feminism, Subjectivity, and the Angler of the House in the Latin American Novel, 1887-7903*. Penn State UP, 2009.

Lawrence, Lyn Nicole. ""Sarah Grand, George Egerton and the Eugenic Social Debate: Marriage, Civic Motherhood, and the New Woman writer." *English Literature in Transition, 1880-1920*. vol. 62, no. 3, 2019, pp. 371-390.

Lefebvre, Henri. *The Production of the Space*. Translated by Donald Nicholson-Smith. Blackwell, 1997.

Leitch, Vincent., B. and Mitchel R. Lewis. "United States." "Cultural Studies." *The John Hopkins Guide to Literary Theory & Criticism*. Edited by Michael Groden, Martin Kreiswirth, and Imre Szeman. The John Hopkins UP, 2005, pp. 229-230.

Lennartz, Norbert. "10 Legends of Infernal Drinkers: Representations of Alcohol in Thomas Hardy and Nineteenth-Century British Fiction." *Drink in the Eighteen and Nineteenth Centuries*. Edited by Susanne Schmid and Barbara Schmidt-Haberkamp, 2014, pp. 115-126.

Lewis, Helene. "Social Darwinism." *The Journal of Psychohistory* vol. 44, no. 2, 2016, pp. 154-161.

Lilienfeld, Jane. "'An Altar to Disease in Years Go By': Alcoholism in *The Major of Casterbridge*. Author Jane Lilienfeld, 1999, pp. 13-84.

Lombroso, Cesare, and William (Enrico) Ferro. *Female Offender* (1895). Philosophical Library, 1958.

——. *The Criminal Woman, the Prostitute, and the Normal Woman*. Translated and edited by Nicole Hahn Rafter and Mary Gibson. Duke UP, 2004.

——. "The Insane Criminal: Special Forms of Criminal Insanity, Alcoholism." *Criminal Man: According to the Classification of Cesare Lombroso*. Montclair, N. J. Patterson Smith, 1972, pp. 74-100.

López, Bago Eduardo. *La prostituta: Novela médico-social*. 1884. Renacimiento Biblioteca de Rescate, 2005.

Magnum, Teresa. *Married Middlebrow, and Militant: Sarah Grand and the New Woman Novel*. The U of Michigan P, 2001.

Manning, Susan, and Andrew Taylor. "Introduction: What is Transatlantic Studies?" *Transatlantic Literary Studies: A Reader*. Edited by Susan Manning & Andrew Taylor. The Johns Hopkins UP, 2007, pp. 1-13.

Marks, Lara. "Medical Care for Pauper Mothers and their Infants: Poor Law Provision and Local Demand in East London, 1870-1929." *Economic History Review*. Vol. 56, no.3, 1993, pp. 518-542.

Mayer, Tamar. "Setting the stage." *Gender Ironies of Nationalism: Sexing the Nation*. Ed. Tamar Mayer. New York: Routledge, 2000, pp. 1-23.

Miller, Gabrielle. *Mapping the Imagination: Feminine Embodiment in the Novels of Benito Pérez Galdós*. University of Virginia, 2015. PhD dissertation. www.libraetd.lib.virginia.edu/public_view/p8418n56z.

Miller, Roy. *Britain and Latin America in the Nineteenth and Twentieth Centuries*. Studies in Modern History, 1993.

Moi, Toril. "What Is a Woman? Sex, Gender, and the Body in Feminist Theory." *What is a Woman? And Other Essays*. Oxford UP, 1999, pp. 3-121.

Morel, B. Augustine. *Traitê des maladies mentales*. Masson, 1860.

Neil, Anna. "The End of the Novel: Naturalism and Reverie in *Tess d'Urbervilles* and in *The Return of the Native.*" *Primitive Minds: Evolution and Spiritual Experience in the Victorian Novel*. The Ohio State UP, 2013, pp. 152-180.

Nunan, Rosanna. "Urban Depravity, Rural Unsophistication: Hereditary Taint in Hardy's *Tess of the D'Urbervilles.*" *Victorian Literature and Culture*. vol. 46, 2018, pp. 289-307.

Ordiz, Javier. "En los márgenes del Naturalismo: mujer, religión y sociedad en Santa, de Federico Gamboa." *Iberoamericana* vol. IX, 35, 2009, pp. 7-17.

"Oxford Dictionaries." *English Oxford Living Dictionaries*, Oxford UP, 2018. https://en.oxforddictionaries.com/definition/deviant.

Pardo Bazán Emilia. *La cuestión palpitante. Obras completas* 1883. Tomo 3, 1957, pp. 574-647.

———. *La gota de sangre.* 191. *Obras completas* Tomo 1. Aguilar, 1964, pp. 275-349.

———. *La piedra angular.* 1891. *Obras completas* Tomo 2. Aguilar, 1957, pp. 994-1014.

———. "Tío terrones." *Obras completas* 1920. Tomo 2, Aguilar, 1957, pp. 1354-1355.

Patterson, Orlando. *Slavery and Social Death: A Comparative Study*. Harvard UP, 1982.

Piccato, Pablo. "Urbanistas, Ambulantes, and Mendigos: The Dispute of Urban Space in Mexico City, 1890-1930." *Reconstructing Criminality in Latin America*. Edited by Carlos A. Aguirre and Robert Buffington. A Scholarly Resources, Inc., 2000, pp. 113-148.

Pirone, Frank. "Introduction." *Female Offender* (1895). Philosophical Library, 1958.

Pizer, John. *The Idea of World Literature: History and Pedagogical Practice*. Louisiana State UP, 2006.

Plotz, Clarke M. "Life in Dead Things: Unreading Memorials in Thomas Hardy's *Tess of the D'Urbervilles. Dickens Studies Annual: Essays on Victorian Fiction*, vol. 50, no. 1, 2019, pp. 106-129.

Pollard, Percival. "The Unlikely Awakening of a Married Woman." *The Awakening* (1899): *A Norton Critical Edition*. Edited by Margo Culley. Norton & Company, 1994, pp. 179-181.

Rafter, Nicole Hann, and Mary Gibson. "Introduction." *Criminal Woman, the Prostitute, and the Normal Woman*. Translated and Edited by Nicole Hahn Rafter and Mary Gibson. Duke UP, 2004.

Rama, Angel. *La ciudad letrada*. Arca, 1984.

Ramé, Louis Marie "Ouida". "The New Woman." *The American New Woman Revisited.* Edited by Martha H. Patterson. Rutgers UP, 2008, pp. 71-1-77.

Rich, Charlotte J. *Transcending the New Woman: Multiethnic Narratives in the Progressive Era.* U of Missouri P, 2009.

Richardson, Angelique. *Love and Eugenics in Late Nineteen Century: Rational Reproduction and the New Woman.* Oxford UP, 2003.

Rodríguez, G. Yilana. "¿Cómo se leyó "Santa,"de Federico Gamboa? Algunos apuntes sobre su recepción." *Revista Crítica Literaria Latinoamericana,* vol. 40, no. 80, 2014, pp. 395-410.

Said Edward. "Yeats and Decolonization." *Nationalism, Colonialism, and Literature.* Edited by Seamus Deane. U of Minnesota P, 1990, pp. 69-98.

———. "Orientalism." *The Norton Anthology of Theory and Criticism.* Edited by Vincent B. Leitch as General Editor. E.W. Norton Company, 2010, pp. 1866-1888.

Sainz Robles de, Federico. "Estudio Preliminar: Su vida." *Obras Completas* vol. 1. Aguilar, 1964, pp. 9-37.

Seitler, Dana. "Introduction." *Atavistic Tendencies: The Culture of Science in American Modernity.* U of Minnesota P, 2008, pp. 1-30.

Sexton, Jay. *The Monroe Doctrine.* Hill Wang, 2011.

Shires, Linda M. "The radical aesthetic of *Tess of the d'Urbervilles.*" *The Cambridge Companion to Thomas Hardy.* Edited by Dale Kramer, Cambridge UP, 1999, pp. 145-163.

Showalter, Elaine, *Sexual Anarchy: Gender and Culture at the Fine-de-Siècle.* Penguin Books, 1990.

Siebenschuh, William., R. "Hardy and the Imagery of Place." *SEL Studies in English Literature 1500-1900,* vol. 39, no. 39, Autum, 1999, pp. 773-789.

Siegfried, William. "The Formation of the Human Psyche." *Athene Noctua: Undergraduate Philosophy Journal,* Issue no. 2, 2014, pp. 1-3.

Slettedahl, Macpherson Heidi. *Transatlantic Women's Literature.* Edinburgh UP, 2008.

Smith, Armantine., M. "The History of the Women's Suffrage Movement in Louisiana." *Louisiana Law Review,* vol. 62, no. 2, 2002, pp. 509-560.

Sutherland, John. "Is Alec a Rapist?" *Heathcliff a Murderer – Puzzles in 19th Century Fiction.* Oxford UP, 1996, pp. 202-212.

Tan Francis, Andrew., Cheryl Tan, and Ruhan Zhang. "School Spirit: Exploring the Long-Term Effects of the U.S. Temperance Movement on Educational Attainment. *Economics of Education Review,* vol. 62, 2018, pp. 162-169.

Thornton, John K. *A Cultural History of the Atlantic World, 1250-1820.* Cambridge UP, 2012.

Tolliver, Joyce. *Cigar Smoke and Violent Water: Gendered Discourse in the Stories of Emilia Pardo Bazán.* Bucknell UP, 1999.

Toner, Deborah. "Medicine, Madness, and Modernity in Porfirian Mexico: Alcoholism as the National Disease." *Alcohol and Nationhood in Nineteenth-Century Mexico.* U of Nebraska P, 2015, pp. 189-256.

Toth, Emily. "A New Bibliographical Approach." Edited by Margo Culley. Norton & Company.1994, pp. 113-119.

Tsuchiya, Akiko. *Marginal Subjects: Gender and Deviance in Fin-de-siécle Spain.* U of Toronto P 2011.

Venegas, Jessica S. "Heterotopic Space the Limits of Naturalist Discourse in Federico Gamboa's *Santa.*" *Symposium,* vol. 64, no 3, 2010, pp. 251-264.

Walkowitz, Judith. *City of Dreadful Delight: Narratives of Sexual Danger in Late-Victorian London.* U of Chicago P, 1992.

Walter, Susan. "Images of the *Femme Fatale* in Two Short Stories by Emilia Pardo Bazán." *Romance Notes,* vol. 55 no. 2, pp. 177-189.

Watts, Cedric. "Hardy's Sue Bridehead and the New Woman." *Critical Survey* vol. 5, no. 2, 1993, pp. 152-156.

Weisbuch, Robert. "Cultural Time in America." *Transatlantic Studies: A Reader.* Edited by Susan Manning and Andrew Taylor. The Johns Hopkins UP, 2007, pp. 97-104.

Williams, Melanie. "Is Alec a Rapist? Cultural Connotations of Rape and Seduction: A Response to Professor John Sutherland." *Feminist Legal Studies,* vol. 7, 1999, pp. 299-316.

Windle, Bertram C. A. *The Wessex of Thomas Hardy.* John Lane the Bodley. Head LTD. 1925.

Witherow, Jean. "Abysses of Solitude: Chopin's Intertextuality with Flaubert" *Mississippi Quarterly: The Journal of Southern Cultures,* Vol. 64 1-2, 2011, pp. 87-113.

Yamin, Rebecca. "Wealthy, Free, and Female: Prostitution in Nineteenth Century New York." *Historical Archeology* vol. 39, no. 1, 2003, pp. 4-18.

Zalduono, María. "Introducción." *La hija del bandido o los subterráneos del nevado* 1887. Stockcero, 2007.

Zola, Émile. *Nana.* 1880. Oxford World Classics, 2009.

———. *The Experimental Novel.* The Cassell Publishing, 189.

Index

Milton Keynes UK
Ingram Content Group UK Ltd.
UKHW022030081223
434064UK00013B/128/J